D1094330

MUZZY

Books by Charles W. Thayer

NONFICTION

Muzzy

Guerrilla

Diplomat

The Unquiet Germans

Bears in the Caviar

Hands Across the Caviar

Russia (with the editors of *Life*)

FICTION

Checkpoint

Moscow Interlude

T. IRONS

MUZZY

by Charles W. Thayer

HARPER & ROW, PUBLISHERS

NEW YORK

 For information address Harper & Row, Publishers, Incorporated, 49 East 33rd Street, New York, N.Y. 10016.

FIRST EDITION

LIBRARY OF CONGRESS CATALOG CARD NUMBER: 66-16629

E-Q

Contents

Introduction

WHEN MY MOTHER DIED in 1964, her English friends held a memorial service for her simultaneously with the funeral at the Church of the Good Shepherd in Bryn Mawr. During the service, the choir sang a passage from the Book of Proverbs, Chapter 31. "It seems to us," an English friend explained, "that it was written for Muzzy."

Who can find a virtuous woman? for her price is far above rubies. The heart of her husband doth safely trust in her, so that he shall have no need of spoil. She will do him good and not evil all the days of her life. She seeketh wool, and flax, and worketh willingly with her hands. . . .

She riseth also while it is yet night, and giveth meat to her household, and a portion to her maidens. . . .

She girdeth her loins with strength, and strengtheneth her arms. . . .

She layeth her hands to the spindle, and her hands hold the distaff. She stretcheth out her hand to the poor; yea, she reacheth forth her hands to the needy. She is not afraid of the snow for her household: for all her household are clothed with scarlet. She maketh herself coverings of tapestry; her clothing is silk and purple. Her husband is known in the gates, when he sitteth among the elders of the land. . . .

Strength and honour are her clothing; and she shall rejoice in time to come. She openeth her mouth with wisdom; and in her tongue is the law of kindness. She looketh well to the ways of her household, and eateth not the bread of idleness. Her children arise up, and call her blessed; her husband also, and he praiseth her. Many daughters have done virtuously, but thou excellest them all. Favour is deceitful, and beauty is vain: but a woman that feareth the LORD, she shall be praised. Give her of the fruit of her hands; and let her own works praise her in the gates.

C.W.T.

Clover Mill House
Chester Springs, Pennsylvania
January, 1966

ONE

The End of Innocence

We were late, of course, getting started. There had been the usual delay assembling five of us children. The sixth, George, was already at Franklin Field presumably struggling nervously into his football uniform. Then there was trouble cranking up the Model T and the usual argument about where each of us was to sit.

Just as we were about to set off, Augustus, the butler, hobbled rheumatically out from "the back" and announced that Aunt Bessie was on the phone. There was an anguished groan from us children. Patiently Muzzy got out and went to the phone. Knowing we were in for a long session, we followed her and took turns listening in on the pantry phone while Aunt Bessie passed on the contents of a letter she had just received from one of the English contingent of the family. Cousin Joe, she reported, was back in Wormwood Scrubs for passing a dud check. Muzzy received the news with little moans of sympathy.

"Not again!" she said incredulously. "But he just got out last month. Another check? . . . Oh." After a long pause, Aunt Bessie reported that one of the nieces was expecting or, as the Wheeler girls delicately said in their private language, "having." Since babies were one of Muzzy's hobbies, this news almost made up for the jailing of Joe. After an interminable discussion about the health and welfare of the rest of the family, Muzzy hung up, promising to continue the discussion when they met for tea after the game.

We clambered back into the Ford and with a roar of the engine and a splatter of gravel we set off. Once on the main road, Muzzy pulled the gas lever under the steering gear down as far as it would go and we sped along at a good twenty-five miles an hour. Always erect, she occasionally leaned forward to ease the strain on the engine as though it were a horse. She wore a wide straw hat from under which wisps of her blond hair streamed in the breeze. Her face was tense, her slightly turned-up nose pink in the cold autumn wind.

We were halfway to town and making good time when an odd sound of rasping metal rose from the floor boards. We children exchanged anxious glances, but Muzzy ignored it. Speaking to no one in particular, she said, "Poor Joe! He's so plucky!" It was not entirely clear whether Joe was plucky for trying to pass bad checks or for taking his jail sentence like a gentleman.

Preoccupied by the strange noises coming from under the car, we children remained silent.

At last the angry clatter got so loud that even Muzzy could not ignore it entirely.

"Get out and see if you can find out what's wrong," she said to me, her eyes still glued to the road, her hands clutching the wheel as though it were the reins of a runaway team.

I waited a moment and then asked anxiously, "Are you going to stop?"

"We can't stop now," Muzzy said apologetically. "We'd miss the kickoff."

Gingerly I crawled out onto the running board and while my sisters held my feet I leaned over, my head inches from the bumpy road. The noise was louder than ever but I could see nothing unusual on the Ford's bottom. Still hanging upside down, I passed the word back to Muzzy. She ordered me back into the car and gave a determined yank on the gas lever as though she might get an extra spurt of speed out of the engine.

"If you can't see anything," she said flatly, "there can't be much wrong."

A few minutes later, with a grinding clatter that scattered the policemen around the stadium, we drew up to the gate and piled out. Muzzy headed for our box at a fast lope, we children following at a full gallop.

We were still milling about trying to settle ourselves when the players kicked off. A few spectators behind us, obviously "out-of-towners," as Muzzy called them, complained that we were blocking their view, but the rest, accustomed to our ways, merely smiled patiently.

The stadium was packed and the crowds were tense, for this was, after all, the big game with Penn's traditional rival, Cornell. Traditional, that is, since the traditional rivalry with Princeton had been interrupted many years before. According to my uncles, that rivalry had ended when one of the Philadelphia Rosengarten twins bit the other Rosengarten twin in the fanny during a scrimmage. In those days football players did not dress up in armor like medieval knights, and the bite, it was reported, was deep and painful. It is still not entirely clear which Rosengarten bit which (we Penn rooters always claimed it was the Princeton twin), but in the ensuing controversy public opinion became so inflamed over this barbaric violation of one of the few football rules then in force that all athletic relations between the universities were severed, and peace had still not been restored decades later.

The Penn-Cornell game that year was bitterly fought, though I can't remember who won. Brother George, playing end, was captain of the Penn team, so naturally feelings ran high in our box. The game was almost over when Penn was forced to punt on a fourth down. George and his fellow end, a brawny Philadelphian called Scull, raced down the field under the kick, and as the Cornell back caught the ball, they hurtled through the air and brought him down with a crash you could hear in the topmost stands. Just to be sure he didn't move again, the rest of the Penn team leapt on the heap.

When the players eventually disentangled themselves, one lone body was lying flat and obviously unconscious on the ground. The referee signaled for the Penn stretcher and as the first-aid squad hurried out onto the field a deep moan rose from the spectators.

My mother, a little nearsighted, turned to a man in the next box and asked whom the body belonged to.

"It's your son George," the man replied glumly.

"Thank heavens!" Muzzy cried out. "I thought it was that poor Scull boy. He's so frail."

"Pluck" was one of Muzzy's favorite words and she not only displayed it herself but demanded it of all of us. She considered frailty of the spirit one of the seven deadly sins. She could tolerate physical frailty in outsiders like Scull but within the family it was permanently outlawed. If we broke an arm or crushed a finger in a door, her remedy for the tears that followed was simple: "Just don't think about it and it will go away."

She would not tolerate any whimpering even in the machines about her and when the Ford complained aloud she dismissed the complaint with contempt. When she had a headache—and she frequently had what we called "splitters"—she surreptitiously took an aspirin and kept silent. If the Ford didn't have the competence to do the equivalent, let it suffer! If the pain was due to lack of grease or oil or water, the car should learn to do without. In fact it was only after she had burned out the engine of one Ford that she learned cars needed water at all. "I thought it only needed gasoline," she said as the red-hot motor expired with a hiss.

When it came to sports, the ability to win was second only to pluck. To her a bad loser was beneath contempt, but a good loser rated little higher. Fiercely competitive, she had always played all out to win. When old age finally sidelined her and she was demoted to being referee, she was just as militant. If one of her family was competing, she considered it her duty to give him the breaks. And when her children competed among themselves, she solved the dilemma by applying the law of primogeniture. Whenever my older brother and I were playing a savage game of croquet, she invariably looked the other way when George kicked his ball into position or pushed my ball away from the wicket. When Cousin Joe lost his game with the London police, she was upset because she felt it was partly her fault. If she'd been there, she'd have found some way to have him win.

As children we all followed her example as best we could and whether it was a game or an argument we competed madly. We even competed in cooking lessons. When my sisters and their neighbors were being taught to cook, they naturally divided into teams, my sisters on one side, the neighbors on the other. Once the competition involved making mayonnaise. I as a child of five was not allowed to participate but I could watch. I observed nervously as the ingredients were poured into the two bowls and the girls began to beat the mixture. Scampering from one bowl to the other, I watched their progress with mounting anxiety because I saw that the neighbors' bowl was thickening faster than my sisters'.

Frantic, I raced back and forth between them. At last it became apparent that unless drastic action was taken my sisters would lose the game—and that, according to family law, was out of the question. But what could I, scarcely tall enough to peer into the bowls, do about it? And then I suddenly realized where my duty lay. Filling my mouth with saliva, I spat violently into the neighbors' bowl. I suffered a rather severe loss of status in the neighborhood thereafter, but my sisters had won and that was the object of the exercise.

As a girl, Muzzy's favorite sport was fox hunting. She hunted with the Radnor Hunt Club and, as always, she competed recklessly. According to her contemporaries, she achieved her greatest triumph when she was still in her late teens.

The members of the hunt had just finished a strenuous day galloping over the countryside and were relaxing over tea in the clubhouse, the ladies in their black riding habits and top hats, the gentlemen in their pink coats. The talk turned to Muzzy's prize mare Black Bess, who had led the field much of the day. One of Muzzy's admirers was praising the mare extravagantly. He was, he said, willing to bet that Black Bess could jump the five-foot gate out of the club's muddy courtyard. A more skeptical member expressed his doubts and soon bets were flying about the room. But when all the bets had been laid, one question remained unasked and unanswered: who was going to ride the mare over the gate? There was an awkward silence among the men. Then Muzzy rose, ordered her tired horse resaddled and, when a groom had brought the mare around, climbed back into her sidesaddle and quietly adjusted her skirt. Then she rode into the yard, ordered the gate closed and, to the astonishment of the stableboys, put Black Bess to it. She had only a few feet of slippery mud for a run but according to eyewitnesses, some of whom were still tottering about town seventy years later, she sailed over easily. Her wide skirt flapped in the breeze and some strands of blond hair streamed out behind her as they always did, but her top hat never shifted its cocky pose.

The rolling fields and woods over which Muzzy and her friends hunted had originally been inhabited by Indians known as Lenapes ar Delawares. William Penn, who founded the colony, admired the Lenapes greatly. "In liberality," he wrote, "they excel: nothing is too good for their friends. . . . The most merry creatures they live, feast and dance perpetually. . . . We sweat to live, their pleasure feeds them: I mean their hunting, fishing and fowling, and this table is spread everywhere."

Whereupon for an undisclosed quantity of beads, castoff clothing and worn-out flintlocks, he relieved them of a large tract of their bounteous territory. By the latter half of the nineteenth century, part of the tract had become the Main Line and the inhabitants, or at least the more fortunate among them, merely sought to combine the two ways of life of which Penn wrote—the Indians' and the English settlers'. Part of their time they spent sweating in their banks and law offices and the rest feasting, dancing, hunting and fishing on their estates.

The extent to which they succeeded can perhaps best be judged by the envy they inspired among those—chiefly out-of-towners—who have sought to describe Philadelphia and the goings on among Main Line families since the turn of the century.

To hear them tell it, one gets the impression of a score or so of fossilized old families playing at lords and ladies barricaded behind the pales of their neo-feudal baronies from which all but the elect were strictly excluded.

Some Philadelphians were incensed at these descriptions by outsiders looking in, but Muzzy dismissed them contemptuously as "trash." The only thing that being an old Philadelphia family signified, she said, was having the knack of holding on to one's ancestors' money—a trait to which she herself ascribed little virtue and which she seldom practiced.

To be sure, there were members of some families who made apes of themselves by gamboling about their family trees but they were in the minority. And anyway what was a Philadelphia family? For generations they had intermarried incessantly if not incestuously. There was hardly a family, for example, that the Biddles could not boast of having infiltrated at one time or another. Others like the Wistars and the Wisters could not even agree on how to spell their family name. And if, as Muzzy stoutly denied, there was a Philadelphia social hierarchy, how would one rank someone called Thayer Dixon in relation to one called Dixon Thayer?

Furthermore, the Main Line was not as some claimed a social barony but a highly successful real-estate speculation on the part of the men who ran the Pennsylvania

Railroad. After the merry Lenapes had been driven out by the white settlers, the area had been in the hands of farmers until the end of the Civil War. A railroad of sorts called the Columbia had been built through it connecting Philadelphia with the Pennsylvania Canal, which provided transportation all the way to Pittsburgh. Originally the rolling stock had consisted of wagons and carriages with flanged wheels pulled by horses. Their average speed was about four miles an hour.

Around 1832 the Columbia acquired some steam locomotives. But even the steam engine had its growing pains—especially on rainy days. Then the great iron contraptions from the Baldwin Locomotive Works roared and belched steam and smoke, but their wheels spun helplessly on the slippery tracks while the horses and their friends whinnied with scornful delight. So whenever the weather was bad, the locomotives were sent back to their barns and the horses once more took over. But then someone invented a way of sanding the tracks and the horses were retired from the railroad for good.

Though horses managed to hold their own for another generation on the roads, their replacement on the railroad marked the beginning of the end of the Age of Innocence and the dawn of the Machine Age. It was also the dawn of some of the fortunes that eventually made the Main Line what it was in Muzzy's days.

In 1857 the Pennsylvania Railroad bought out the Columbia but for some time continued to run only through trains to the West, which stopped briefly at what was then called Humphreysville for fuel and water. There were half a dozen trains a day but they were generally filled with newly arrived immigrants from Europe seeking their fortunes in the West—hardly the type Philadelphia lawyers and merchants wanted to rub shoulders with.

But then someone in the PRR had the original idea of developing the Main Line, as it was already called, as a suburb—or, as he expressed it, a summer resort. This was based on the obvious speculation that Philadelphians might prefer the open country and rolling hills to the hot and fetid streets of the city, at least during the summer months. The inducement the railroad offered was frequent commuter service free of undesirable immigrants.

But before they publicly announced the inauguration of the Paoli Local, the gentlemen of the railroad and their friends, whom they generously let into their secret, took the precaution of buying up a large number of farms along the route from farmers who little suspected the spectacular rise in land values the development would bring. Among their friends was Charles Wheeler, my grandfather, a Philadelphia banker who bought himself a large farm in Bryn Mawr. Fifty years later they might all have gone to jail for their scheming, but in those days a freer standard of ethics prevailed and the Congress was less concerned with protecting the interests of unsuspecting farmers against the city slickers.

By no means all the farmers sold out and today many of the most widely known names on the Main Line are those of families that owned land there long before the Pennsylvania Railroad was ever dreamed of. Rowland Ellis, for example, a descendant of the first farmer in the area, after whose farm Bryn Mawr was named, still owns a farm nearby.

The speculators—or perhaps we should call them innovators—were anxious to maintain a high standard for their summer resort and, doubtless unaware of the precedent they were setting, ruled that no one buying lots in the choicer sections should build a mansion, as they called it, costing less than $8,000 and in the less choice areas $5,000.

Since the farms the developers bought and the lots they sold were on both sides of the tracks, the Main Line subsequently became known as the only place where it didn't matter which side of the tracks you were born on.

As a final touch to lend class to the development, the railroad directors, catering to the anglophilia of well-to-do Philadelphians, named the stations of the Main Line after Welsh and English towns. Humphreysville, the only large village, they renamed Bryn Mawr just before Uncle Charlie was born there, making him Bryn Mawr's first-born citizen. There were a few exceptions. They called the end of the line Paoli after a then popular Italian general and freedom fighter. For some odd reason they named the place where I was born Villa Nova, possibly because they hoped it too would develop into a flourishing new town. And when eventually they found it cheaper to spell the name Villanova, the old inhabitants objected vigorously but futilely. Probably to compensate for the un-Englishness of Villa Nova, Muzzy named our place Kyneton after the village in Gloucestershire whence the Thayers originally emigrated. (Daddy, who was no anglophile, liked to point out that Kyneton was actually the Old English version of "Cowtown.")

The PRR enjoyed a monopoly of freight and passenger traffic that was challenged only by the horse-drawn traffic on the Lancaster Pike, the old wagon route to the West. But even that competition seemed too much for the railroad directors. So a number of them, including Mr. Alexander J. Cassatt, formed a private company and bought the pike, which had been improved at vast public expense, for $9,000 from the government and converted it into a private toll road. Not only did it curb competition but it proved a highly lucrative investment until 1917 when it was again made public property.

While the directors of the railroad seemed unconcerned with the public interest, they were much more solicitous of their friends, on whom they bestowed such privileges as they seemed entitled to as a class. One of the privileges they distributed to their friends was the use of passes on the turnpike, and as a child I can recall our coachmen proudly shouting out the name of their masters as they sped past a tollhouse.

On the railroad, too, privileges were widely distributed, varying in degree. For example, the early-morning

Paoli Local invariably waited at Merion Station, where my Thayer grandparents lived, until my father and his four brothers were all safely aboard.

When my uncles grew up and in turn became officials of the railroad, they were given passes on all trains. But, according to the rules, pass holders, known as "deadheads," were obliged to stand if there were no seats for ticket holders. Uncle Walter, who developed varicose veins when he grew older and hated to stand, got around the rule by always carrying a regular ticket, which he surrendered only if a ticket holder challenged his deadhead status.

But to us children the supreme privilege was enjoyed by our cousins the Morrises, who had a big place just west of Villa Nova Station. There they built their own station platform and evoked the privilege of flagging down any train that suited their fancy whether it was the Paoli Local or the Broadway Limited bound for Chicago.

Some of the Main Line stations eventually developed into flourishing villages and towns. But Villa Nova, despite its name, remained a stunted rural stop. It had no shops, no stores, not even a filling station during my day.

All it had was a ticket office and post office combined. They were both run by a pair of elderly sisters, the Misses Gleason, who held the community in thrall since they controlled not only admission to the Paoli local but also could by simply slamming shut the post-office window withhold your daily mail and even your Philadelphia *Public Ledger*.

As children we were terrified of both Miss Gleasons (we could never tell them apart) for though they could be most amiable they sometimes kept you waiting for hours while they tried to figure the cost of a ticket or find the mail.

Not until they were retired was their mysteriously erratic behavior explained. At that time neither the U.S. government nor the PRR was particularly generous toward pensioners. When the ladies of Villa Nova learned how little the two old spinsters were to receive for the rest of their lives, they banded together and raised a handsome pension fund. Not long afterward the ladies learned what everyone else had known for years—the dear old girls were quietly drinking themselves to death on their new affluence. The ladies were scandalized and Muzzy asked one of the Irish maids at Kyneton whether or not the story was true:

"Sure, Madam, and I cood ha told ye when ye was getting that money together the bawth of them were boozers," she said with a leer.

Villa Nova boasted one other public institution: McGrady, the hack driver. From sunup to nightfall, except when on a rare job, he dozed on the box of his hack. Even when he slept, McGrady's jaws were always in motion chewing his daily cud of tobacco, his moth-eaten, battered top hat rising and falling rhythmically, while his horse's hind legs stomped intermittently in the pile of horse manure in the middle of the gravel circle of the station McGrady had pre-empted.

The hack was a station carriage. (Not until the car age did we hear the expression "station wagon.") It was a black leather box on four wheels with a single window, which seldom opened, in the rear door. Inside it smelt of a combination of musty ancient upholstery, horse and human sweat, and McGrady's chewing tobacco. Fortunately, we seldom rode with McGrady because the twenty-five cents he charged to take us the mile to Kyneton was considered exorbitant even by our richer neighbors. While we children walked the mile to catch the train taking us to school, our parents were usually driven in their own station carriage, which smelt a good deal less disagreeable than McGrady's although it too was lightless, airless, and windowless, except for the back window that, like McGrady's, was seldom opened. One of my sisters with a tendency toward seasickness had only to look at the station carriage to "fwo up."

But the drive to the station was the universal practice for all the men of the community who went to town daily to attend to their affairs.

The Paoli Local's facilities did not always enhance these affairs and Daddy sometimes suggested that some of the commuters would have been better advised to stay home and let their hired help run their business. However, in nineteenth-century Quaker-dominated Philadelphia, idlers no matter what their financial status were ranked with anarchists, socialists and atheists.

The husband of one of my aunts who lived with my

grandmother at Pembroke in Bryn Mawr was a regular commuter. Although it was considered a dark secret from the general public, we nephews and nieces as we grew up discovered to our dismay that he had no office in Philadelphia, no business to run, no affairs to supervise. Nevertheless, in conformity with local custom he was driven each morning around eleven to Bryn Mawr Station, where he boarded the Paoli Local.

Once in town, he headed for the one place he had to go to—his club. There he had a cocktail or two and a substantial lunch and played a few hands of bridge. Then, his affairs attended to, he walked to Broad Street Station, buying a pink carnation for his buttonhole on the way. Back at my grandmother's home he would retire for his nap and re-emerge a little late for tea, elegantly turned out in a black coat, striped trousers and carnation.

With a baleful eye he would study the tea table, remark acidly that the Thayer children had evidently been there before him, and thereupon ring for the butler to bring his Scotch-and-soda.

Once he was being sued by some poor person who had had the misfortune to be run over by his carriage. When he appeared at the courthouse wearing his carnation as usual, his lawyer rushed up to him and whispered, "Take that damn flower out of your buttonhole." My uncle haughtily ignored the warning, strode pompously into the courtroom carnation and all—and lost the suit.

Like other younger ladies of the community, Muzzy often drove her own carriage, and when she went to visit the Miss Haughtons eight miles away, she sometimes drove the tandem, one of the most difficult but speedy rigs of the horse-drawn age. I still remember sitting with her on the box, the two horses racing along at a fast trot, keeping a good ten miles an hour.

A few cars had already made their appearance by the time I was born and the fear they produced in the horses usually made it necessary for the car driver to stop and switch off his engine until the horses had passed. Those who did not were classified as bounders and were not invited to dinner.

Muzzy and Daddy's first experience with a horseless carriage was an unhappy one. They had been given the car (I don't know what make it was) by my Uncle Alec Wheeler as a wedding present. Neither of them was particularly thrilled by the gadget and seldom used it except to drive to my grandmother's for Sunday family supper. My father called it the "try-weekly" auto trip. The first attempt ended fortunately at the foot of the Kyneton drive so they were able to hitch up a carriage and arrive not too late for dinner. The second attempt, some weeks later, got them about a mile down the Gulph Road before Daddy, who was an expert at swearing, walked home for the carriage. Muzzy said he was cursing until he got out of earshot and John Nagle, the coachman, says he heard him coming two hundred yards away. The third trip, which ended near enough to my grandmother's to permit them to walk through the rain to supper, was the last.

A year or two after their unhappy experience,

Daddy, who was then assistant manager of Cramps Shipyard, was offered the management of one of the many motor companies springing up all over the East. It was a tempting offer. The factory was at Ardmore, only four stations up the line from Villa Nova, whereas Cramps was far away in North Philadelphia, which required both a Paoli Local ride and another long streetcar ride up Broad Street. It was also a promotion and the salary, I daresay, was an improvement.

But Daddy hesitated. As a marine engineer he recognized and indeed welcomed the steamship. Ships were as old as history and steamships were simply an improvement over sailing vessels or oars. He also recognized the steam locomotive. In fact he had spent a summer when he was a college student as a stoker on a PRR train to Pittsburgh. But the automobile was different. First of all, it was a short-haul affair. What could it do that a horse couldn't? Secondly, he knew from his experience with the Wedding Present that it was unreliable. And finally, what future did it have?

Daddy did not make decisions lightly. For several days he brooded and then one Sunday he went up to "the Corner," a main-road intersection near Kyneton, armed with a pencil and notebook. He sat down on a grassy knoll overlooking the crossing and every time a carriage went by he put down a check. Every time a car passed, he put down an "X." For three hours each Sunday thereafter, Daddy conducted his personal poll on the future of the motorcar. After several weeks he totaled up the checks and the "X"s. Then he went off by himself to think it over and at last he came home his mind made up. He would stay on at Cramps, he told Muzzy. The automobile, he had decided, was a passing fad.

TWO

Those Wheelers

DURING THE LATTER HALF of the nineteenth century when Muzzy was a child, Philadelphia society modeled itself largely on the English socially, sartorially, in sports and even (alas!) gastronomically. Whenever possible the men bought their clothes in Savile Row and had their hunting and polo boots made at Peal's. They played English games as nearly as they could understand the English rule books. In football, they went pretty far wrong but in cricket, polo, tennis, and the hunting field they copied their cousins to the letter.

And when the PRR offered them country places, they built them like English country mansions and stocked them with English or Irish servants.

So when Grandfather Wheeler built Pembroke, he faithfully copied British Victorian styles. The house was built of rough-hewn stone with many steep gables and dormer windows. Subsequently my grandmother added a pretentious portico complete with crenelated walls.

Inside, the ground floor had high ceilings to cope with summer heat and a paneled hall so dark you never knew if you were getting into the right coat. In one corner was a player piano, which you pumped with your feet and which played tunes from perforated rolls. There was also a Victorian drawing room but children were not allowed in it and I have only the vaguest impression of lots of fragile bibelots and abominably uncomfortable furniture.

The room I remember best was the library where tea was served. It was designed in the best Victorian baronial tradition with an enormous brick fireplace set in a niche occupying one end of the long room. The walls were paneled in dark oak and above the paneling was a fascinating array of moose and buffalo heads, elephant tusks, polar-bear and tiger skins and African spears arranged like sunbursts, which my uncles had thoughtfully brought home to my grandmother from Alaska, Africa and India.

I hardly remember the upper stories because tea was never served there and the only times I ever lived at Pembroke were when my sisters or brother were having mumps or measles at Kyneton. As I invariably got the mumps or the measles promptly and was sent home, my stays at Pembroke were brief.

The house was set in the midst of endless lawns studded with copper beeches—the arboreal hallmark of

Victorian landscaping by which you can still date any garden in Europe or America. There was also a formal terraced garden with Italian statuary, fountains and goldfish ponds.

Every spring the Wheeler family packed their belongings at their town house on Walnut Street into a couple of large vans each drawn by four dray horses. (The PRR did not stoop to short-haul freight.) Then the family would take the Paoli Local to Bryn Mawr and drive to Pembroke, half a mile from the station.

It was an exciting day for the Wheeler children because they were allowed to have a picnic lunch, served from wicker hampers by the servants. But by far the most exciting part of it was that first night at Pembroke when they were permitted to sleep on the floor since the horse vans carrying the mattresses always arrived after bedtime.

As the service on the Paoli Local improved, Pembroke became the year-round home of the family and in summer, following the tribal migrations then in fashion, the Wheelers moved to Newport.

Grandfather Wheeler had begun his career in the family iron foundry of Morris, Tasker & Co., later Morris, Wheeler & Co., which as the family always pointed out with pride had forged the iron chain that was strung across the Hudson to keep out the British fleet during the Revolution. Nearly two hundred years later it performed a similar public service by making and installing steel beams to prop up the sagging roof of

Independence Hall. Grandfather subsequently became a banker and when he died was a director of half the banks in Philadelphia.

In 1883 Grandfather Wheeler was coming home from Newport with his son Charles. The train was late getting into New York City and he had to hurry to catch the ferry to Jersey City. As he ran down Vesey Street, he had a heart attack and died on the spot.

Granny Wheeler had been brought up a strict Quaker and when she married an Episcopalian her parents refused to attend the wedding ceremonies on religious grounds. All their married lives my grandparents called each other in public "Mr. Wheeler" and "Mrs. Wheeler." Records do not show whether this also held on more intimate occasions.

They had eight children, including three sons who dutifully went to St. Paul's School and then to Harvard. However, the university's rolls do not list any of them among its graduates.

For Granny, life with a well-to-do-banker husband must have been a release from the restricted existence of a pious Quaker household. And when she became a widow with a substantial fortune, she promptly shed any lingering vestiges of Quaker frugality.

A devotee of Queen Victoria, her first move was to make her summer home on the Isle of Wight in the English Channel, where she watched the royal regattas with exquisite envy. Most of her children inherited her anglophilia and three of them eventually married Englishmen and settled in England.

But probably the biggest if not the best influence after Grandfather died was her first son-in-law, Dick, a man of great charm and worldly tastes but none of the means to satisfy them. So he persuaded Granny to provide them. At first he even managed her estate, but with such disastrous results that she had to sell off a large part of the Pembroke property to recoup. After that he confined himself to social guidance and the spending of her fortune. It was he who persuaded her to spend her summers in England and her winters—or at least one winter—in Rome, and it was he who brought Count Pappenheim into the family circle. But I'll come to that later.

Though she managed to get her sons in and out of St. Paul's and Harvard, there is little record of any formal schooling for the five girls. When Muzzy was in her eighties, she suddenly claimed she had once attended the Pomfret School for Girls. But as she failed to provide details, we have no way of knowing just what this schooling amounted to.

We do know that she and some of her sisters briefly attended a finishing school in Dresden. But except for a smattering of German and an acute case of homesickness Dresden made little impression.

There were therefore some yawning gaps in Muzzy's education. She could add and subtract a bit and she often tried to multiply and divide with little success. Fractions and percentages were far beyond her ken. On the other hand her English governesses had made her read quantities of English and classical literature with the result that she knew her Walter Scott and her Greek mythology thoroughly. While her mathematical deficiencies caused havoc when, after my father's death, she had to take on all the family accounts, her knowledge of the classics was invaluable to her when she did crossword puzzles or competed in parlor games with the family. If she had had to choose again between the two branches of learning, I'm sure she would have opted for the classics.

As for languages, she could handle French and had learned some German at Dresden. Later when she engaged German governesses to take care of us, her German became much more fluent but never entirely accurate. Nevertheless she liked to use it whenever she could. In fact she was something of a show-off about it.

Once when I was stationed in Germany after the Second World War, I got a letter from her and across the top of the envelope she had written in her large bold handwriting, "*Luftwaffe.*" Somehow the post office figured what she was driving at when she marked the letter with the name of Hitler's air force and they duly delivered it by *Luftpost.*

On another occasion she came to Bonn by train to visit me from Paris where she had been staying with my sister. When I met her at the station, she was deeply upset by the destruction she had seen in the German towns she had passed through. One of the towns just south of Bonn, she said, looked absolutely flat. I asked her which town it was.

"I saw the name on the platform," she said. "It was called Bahnsteig" ("station platform" in German).

Once she came to visit me in Munich when I was Consul General. There one evening we were at a dinner with Crown Prince Rupprecht, the Pretender to the Bavarian throne, and Muzzy was seated next to him. He was about seventy-five at the time and Muzzy was seventy-nine so they struck it off at once, he speaking a smattering of English, she her usual German.

Early on in the conversation she asked him if he had ever known another Bavarian called Max Pappenheim. Rupprecht said he had known him well and that as a young man he had been the biggest roisterer in Munich. Sensing Muzzy's interest in this notorious character, he launched into a series of tales about the dreadful doings of Max, his wild profligacy, his wenching and drinking, his gambling and brawling. Across the table I listened with ears flapping.

We had finished dessert when Rupprecht said, "And when he had run through every penny of his fortune and sold almost all his estates, do you know what he did then?" Muzzy shook her head, waiting to hear Max's worst crime.

"He married an American," Rupprecht said in tones of horror. Then suddenly a worried look came over him.

"But, Madame," he asked. "How did you know Max Pappenheim?"

"He married my sister," Muzzy said, smiling amiably. Just then the hostess gave the signal to rise.

As he left the table, the Crown Prince did an end run

around it, grabbed me by the lapels and shook me furiously. "I saw you listening the whole time and you never stopped me," he remonstrated.

"Sir," I replied, "for every story you told about Uncle Max, my mother has two to match it."

Stories of Uncle Max had filled our childhood: how he had beaten up my uncle for cutting Uncle Max's absurdly long little-finger nail—the barbarous Central European badge of nobility—while he was taking a nap; how he had mulcted the best tailors of London; how he had slept with the servants at Ettal Castle during his honeymoon. But just how he had managed to marry Aunt Nee was seldom touched upon and Muzzy always got vaguer than usual when we pressed her.

During that visit in Munich, however, she had insisted on going back to Ettal, now a boys' school, for she had visited her sister there after the honeymoon. An amiable Benedictine monk let us look about after Muzzy had explained her association with the castle. Afterward we went to the village square and Muzzy went from kiosk to kiosk buying picture postcards. Each time she asked the woman serving her if her parents had ever worked in the castle. Most of them had. When Muzzy emerged from the last kiosk, she was shaking her head dolefully. "I'm afraid it must have been true," she muttered.

"What's true?" I asked.

"About Max's morals," she said. "Every one of those women is the spitting image of him."

Toward the end of Muzzy's visit my wife and I took

her up to a hunting lodge we had high in the Bavarian Alps. It was a cold February weekend and the snow was so deep that we had to have a sledge take us up the mountain, but despite her seventy-nine years Muzzy was delighted by the crisp mountain air and immediately set out on a long walk, plunging vigorously through the snow.

That evening she was tired and had a cocktail before dinner. In the high thin air, it took effect at once and when I offered her a second she eagerly accepted. It was then that I seized the opportunity to ask Muzzy just how Aunt Nee had ever married Max.

"It was during that winter in Rome," Muzzy said.

"Rome? What were you doing in Rome?"

"I don't really know why we were there. It was Dick's idea—to take the family to Rome for a winter." And then she went on to tell the story of the great Roman romance.

At her son-in-law Dick's suggestion Granny had arrived in Rome with her entire family of eight, established herself in a fashionable hotel and even acquired a family doctor, a successful young Swedish physician named Dr. Axel Munthe, who later became famous as the author of *The Story of San Michele,* a book about Capri.

At about the same time, Max Pappenheim, a big ruddy-faced, red-haired, elegantly turned-out young man, made his appearance on the Roman scene. Having run through his fortune and used up his personal credit not only in his native Munich but also in Berlin, Paris and London, there was no other place he could go where tradesmen would keep him in the style to which he had been born.

Somehow or other Max heard about the American widow and her string of daughters. He managed an introduction through our worldly Uncle Dick and carefully looked over the field as he would have looked over a line-up of fillies in the paddock at Ascot. His fancy hit upon the second daughter, Mary, later known to us as Aunt Nee.

She was attractive and tall. She carried herself well and rather looked the part of a countess. But she was dreadfully shy, and, though quite a beauty, was overshadowed by her oldest sister. The young men, put off by her apparent aloofness, left her alone, which only added to the shyness and lack of self-assurance that she hid behind her austere bearing.

Max had picked well, for of all the daughters she was the most ready to respond to advances. The courtship was Teutonically thorough, vigorous and well planned and unlike the Schlieffen Plan, which the German army was then cooking up to conquer France, it quickly conquered Mary. She announced to her mother that she was in love with Max and Max in turn made a formal bid for her hand with all the pomp and formality of a Central European court. Granny was shaken, as she had not planned for Mary to marry quite so young—she was only seventeen. But her efforts to dissuade her were feeble and futile and after all, she argued, if she had to marry, what was better than a German count, except perhaps an English lord?

She consulted her eldest son. Apparently Uncle Charlie had not been entirely taken in by the young Bavarian nobleman's charms. Though he was only nineteen, Charlie was more hardheaded than his mother and thorough in his judgments. He decided that Max would bear a little looking into.

So with a friend, Freddy Allen, who happened to be in Rome, Uncle Charlie took the train to Munich to see what he could find out. His investigations were not difficult; everyone with whom he talked knew Max or his reputation. In fact most of them were either his creditors or his cuckolds.

Armed with enough information to have caused the Mafia to blackball Max, Uncle Charlie and Freddy Allen returned to Rome. They told Granny what they had learned. Granny, rattled by the situation, told Mary. Mary, in love for the first time in her life, flatly refused to believe a word of it and promptly told Max.

Max was understandably upset and annoyed and he acted with characteristic vigor. He challenged Freddy Allen to a duel. There was consternation in the Wheeler household when the invitation arrived. Uncle Charlie pointed out that he had made the investigation and brought the charges, and insisted it was he who should fight the duel. Granny quailed at the thought and Freddy Allen rightly pointed out that Max had challenged him, not Uncle Charlie, and he was going to fight. But how?

As the challenged man, it was up to Allen to choose the weapons, but he had never so much as handled a dueling sword, let alone fight with one. And he was a notoriously bad shot, especially with a pistol, a weapon Max had been brought up with. He was an excellent boxer and not a bad wrestler but neither of these was among the accredited weapons for dueling in Rome in the eighteen-nineties.

While Allen pondered his gloomy future, Granny suddenly had a brilliant idea: she would consult Dr. Munthe, who by now had become not only her physician but her social confidant. He was summoned and informed of the bad news. He listened gravely. It was indeed a most awkward situation, he told Granny. However, he consented to try to smooth things over. For several tense days the Wheelers waited nervously and so did Freddy Allen.

Finally Dr. Munthe reported that he had arranged a compromise. There would be no duel provided Mary married Max. Since Granny knew she could never dissuade her daughter anyway, she joyously accepted. Freddy Allen protested vigorously that his honor was being besmirched, but Uncle Charlie told him they had more important things to worry about and the two of them hurried back by the next ship to Philadelphia. There Uncle Charlie told his uncle, who was Mary's guardian, about Max and with the uncle's help had what money she possessed so tied up in trusts that Max would never see a penny of it. It was the first but not the last time Uncle Charlie tied up funds in trusts. In fact he got so expert that when the 1929 crash came along his sisters almost made a profit out of it.

Meantime Granny and the rest of the family returned

to Philadelphia to prepare for the wedding. Soon Max arrived too and made himself so obnoxious at the Philadelphia Club that he was almost thrown out. He even told about himself the old European boast that water never passed his lips and when asked how he brushed his teeth replied in a heavy German accent:

"For dat I use a light Moselle."

According to the family retainers who witnessed it, Aunt Nee's wedding was a very grand affair. As they described it to us many years later, the carriage carrying the bride and groom back from the Walnut Street church was drawn by six snow-white horses. Muzzy always stoutly denied the part about the horses but we children much preferred the servants' version and for once ignored Muzzy's protests. So the six snow-white horses were firmly established in the family legend.

After the wedding the bride and groom sailed back to Europe for their honeymoon at Ettal Castle, a large sprawling affair in the Bavarian Alps just south of Oberammergau. It was so heavily mortgaged that Uncle Max had to sell it soon afterward. When he discovered what Uncle Charlie had done with Aunt Nee's money, his interest in matrimony waned considerably. So did Aunt Nee's, for other reasons, so she moved to London and lived there for the rest of her life. Though she gave up Max she did not give up his title, and was always known as Countess Pappenheim. As she explained to her sisters, "It's so useful when one goes shopping."

Not believing in divorce, Aunt Nee remained legally married to Max and thus a German citizen. When

World War I broke out, she was by English law an enemy alien, a status she successfully concealed for some time. But then Uncle Charlie in a letter asked her if her German citizenship was causing her difficulties. The censors read the letter, Aunt Nee's status as an enemy alien was uncovered, and thenceforth she was required to report to the police once a week. For the rest of her life she never entirely forgave Uncle Charlie's indiscretion.

Max was less fortunate and was deprived of his title as head of the Pappenheim family, which he made over to his younger brother. Muzzy always claimed he did so to get rid of his debts. However, half a century later I was looking through the library of a Munich friend when I came upon the *Blue Book,* the studbook of Bavarian nobility. I at once looked up Uncle Max and there I read, "Deprived of his title for marrying beneath the family rank."

As Muzzy finished her story, I asked what happened to Max in the end. "Your Uncle Charlie saw him in Shanghai after the war."

"Shanghai?" I asked, astonished.

"Yes, Shanghai. He was selling Australian horses to the Chinese government. You see, Mamma gave him a hundred dollars a month to stay out of America and his brother gave him a hundred marks a month to stay out of Europe. There weren't many other places fit for Max to go to."

Muzzy fell silent, her eyes sad, her face glum.

"Poor Max" she said wistfully. "He wasn't really bad. He was just naughty. He was a fine horseman though his hands were a bit heavy on the reins." She paused, and then she added, her voice gentle with compassion, "And he *was* a good shot."

My own memories of Pembroke date from after World War I. By then Granny Wheeler had been paralyzed by a stroke and though her mind was as active as ever she was a helpless invalid cared for by a trio of nurses. Despite the paralysis she could still talk a little and even wag her right arm up and down on the white bedcover to emphasize her amusement over a joke or her anger when someone annoyed her, which was not seldom.

Each afternoon she was carried downstairs and placed in a hospital bed, either on the enclosed porch at the south side in winter or on the screened porch at the north side in summer. There her children and grandchildren paid court practically daily, lured, at least in the case of the grandchildren, by the tea and sandwiches. Wafer-thin fresh bread with slices of tomato were my favorites.

After the war Aunt Nee made annual pilgrimages to her native land, spending several months at a time at Pembroke.

During her visits she ran the household with a regal hand, finding it hard to conceal her impatience with her less than aristocratic American nieces and nephews. Pembroke's staff was always presided over by an English butler; that is, after Augustus, the former slave boy, was relegated to the less regal establishment at Kyneton.

The first of the English butlers was McConvil, a tall,

cadaverous man who looked as if he would blow away at a harsh word. However, he had far more stamina than most and withstood Aunt Nee's stern discipline without a murmur. His passion in life, aside from presiding over "the back" at Pembroke, was bicycling. He had a big English bike with a three-speed gear that seemed to me the ultimate breakthrough of the Machine Age. Occasionally he would let me ride it around the drive at Pembroke but never off the property. I often heckled Muzzy to try to buy the bicycle from him but she invariably told me that the pony I rode to Haverford School and home again via tea at Pembroke was quite good enough for me.

We Thayers thought McConvil was the grandest of butlers but Aunt Nee evidently had other standards. One evening she was playing bridge with some friends at Pembroke when McConvil appeared and stood silent at her elbow waiting to be recognized. Aunt Nee's face hardened as she tried to concentrate on the cards, ignoring McConvil entirely, apparently on the assumption that if she paid no attention to him he would go away. But McConvil continued to stand there. Aunt Nee went on playing her cards as though he had never existed.

But finally his presence became more than she could stand.

Without so much as looking at him she said firmly, "How often must you be told, McConvil, not to interrupt when we are playing bridge?"

McConvil tipped his body forward submissively. "Yes, Your Ladyship." But he held his ground. Deliberately Aunt Nee played another card. Then again without raising her eyes from the table she said curtly, "Well, then?"

It should have been enough to dismiss an entire army. But McConvil bowed again and repeated, "Yes, Your Ladyship," and remained at her elbow. Finally Aunt Nee lost her patience. She turned on him furiously. "I have told you to leave. Now, go!"

"Yes, Your Ladyship," McConvil said but he did not budge.

Beside herself, she snapped, "Why don't you do as you are told?"

The butler's gaunt frame heaved a sigh of relief. At last he had been given permission to speak:

"Your Ladyship," he said apologetically, "the house is on fire." A moment later the clanging bells of the Bryn Mawr Fire Brigade were heard through the heavy curtains as the big red engine swung into the drive. Actually only one back wing of the house was ablaze and the firemen soon had it out.

When McConvil finally left Pembroke, presumably to die of consumption, his place was taken by Banks. Banks was quite another type, though of course just as English and if anything even more imperious. He was tall, vigorous and exuded an air of complete self-assurance if not superiority, especially toward the grandchildren who made such unseemly pigs of themselves over the sandwiches.

One afternoon a newlywed sister of mine came for tea with her husband. When they were leaving, Banks appeared as usual and silently helped my sister into her coat. When the door had closed behind them, my sister turned to her husband. "That damned Banks!" she exploded. "He always makes me feel like a poor relation."

"And what," her husband asked, "do you think you are?"

On one of her annual visits Aunt Nee invited the Thayer clan to dinner. It was a hot summer evening and the windows were wide open to catch any suspicion of a breeze. Banks and a footman were serving and we were on our best behavior because we were terrified of "the Aunt."

But when a bat darted through the window and began circling the great crystal chandelier above the table, pandemonium broke loose. My sisters, brought up on the well-known fact that bats get into women's hair and infest it with deadly lice, darted under the table. Even Muzzy was shaken, but Aunt Nee sitting stiff and erect at the head of the table never lost her poise. Unfolding a large linen napkin that had been lying on her lap, she carefully put it over her head, completely hiding her face. Then she rang the bell and as Banks appeared with the usual "Yes, Your Ladyship," she said in a sepulchral voice from under her shroud, "Banks, there's a bat in the room. Remove it."

"Yes, Your Ladyship," Banks said as if he had been asked to pass the dessert.

For five minutes there was silence except for the fluttering of the bat and the occasional squeals of my sisters under the table. Meanwhile Aunt Nee sat austere and erect, her head completely draped in the napkin.

Finally there was the sound of doors opening and Banks appeared carrying a tennis racket.

"Your Ladyship?"

"Yes, Banks?" came the voice from under the napkin.

"The bat is secured in the drawing room and I have locked the door."

"Thank you, Banks," she said as she removed her covering and without a tremor of expression resumed her eating.

In those days at least, Philadelphians firmly subscribed to the view that only

> Fools' names and fools' faces
> Always appear in public places.

To have one's picture in the paper or even to be mentioned in public print by name was considered the depth of vulgarity and branded one as a "boor" or—even worse—a "climber." There were of course exceptions to the law of anonymity but they were rigidly limited by custom to such doings as weddings, débuts and funerals. On such occasions the family itself would telephone the social editors of the *Public Ledger* and the *Bulletin* and read a carefully worded announcement to be printed exactly in that form with no additions or alterations. As few families had much journalistic talent, the announcements did not often make very good copy, but rules were rules and if some eager reporter should violate them, he could count on getting a blast from his editor or publisher, who had got the same from the offended party.

However, with the Countess the strain was sometimes

too great for the most disciplined newspaper staff. To have a real native Countess on the Main Line and not exploit her news value was more than some social reporters could bear, and from time to time an item would appear that Countess Pappenheim had arrived from London or had left or had appeared at some function. In such instances Aunt Nee would get livid with anger and rail at the impudence of the American press. In London, so she said, except for mention in the *Court Gazette,* nothing of the sort ever would occur. But later when we began visiting England and reading the English papers, we questioned the accuracy of her boast as we perused accounts in the London press about the scandalous goings on among the nobility.

What worried us more than items in the Philadelphia papers about Aunt Nee were the references to ourselves that appeared only because of our relationship to the Countess:

"Countess Pappenheim's niece Betsy Thayer played center forward for Miss Wright's School yesterday when it was defeated 8–0 by Shipley." Or:

"Countess Pappenheim's sister Mrs. Thayer poured at the Women's Auxiliary of the Church of the Good Shepherd." Or:

"Countess Pappenheim's nephew George Thayer, also present at the wedding, had a black eye said to have been caused by a street scuffle early Sunday morning." Or:

"Countess Pappenheim's niece Mrs. Almy has had another child, her sixth."

Aunt Nee was by no means the only other character

who emerged from the Wheeler brood. Probably the solidest of them all was Uncle Charlie. Brought up in Granny Wheeler's lavish style, from the day he left Harvard (without graduating) he traveled, shot big game and had himself a good time. He played polo at Bryn Mawr, Newport and even in the international tournaments that were just becoming fashionable. He was an excellent player and a keen one. Many years later when I began to play polo at West Point, he came up regularly to watch me. Once he got into conversation with our coach, who very kindly began to explain the intricacies of the game.

Later the coach told me my uncle had caught on very quickly. I smiled and pointed out that he once had an international handicap of eight goals. The coach, whose handicap was a mere five, was not amused.

But as Uncle Charlie grew older, he slowed up and one year his handicap dropped to seven. At about the same time, he began to realize that Granny Wheeler's estate was in very poor shape. Overnight he sold his string of ponies, took over the estate office in Philadelphia and became a model of frugality—a trait he tried vainly to instill in his sisters and brothers. Nevertheless he did manage to recoup his mother's losses, and kept the family solvent despite themselves.

A bachelor for many years, he eventually married a beautiful San Francisco divorcée who after several seasons in Philadelphia tried to persuade him to move to the West Coast. But Uncle Charlie remained loyal to Philadelphia and especially, as its first-born citizen, to Bryn

Mawr. So Auntie, as we called his wife, prevailed on him to build a most elaborate house on the Main Line, complete with an upstairs terraced garden to which laborers had to carry tons of soil and fertilizer in hods up shaky ladders. When it was finished at vast expense, Uncle Charlie's friends, pointing out that his mother's house was called Pembroke and his brother's house in England was Ladbroke, suggested he call his own Charlie's Broke.

But Uncle Charlie kept to his own frugal ways and when he died in 1934 it was on the iron cot he had slept on ever since he had turned his back on the polo-playing set.

Then there was Uncle Stuart, whom I never knew, who died of yellow fever during the Spanish-American War. The youngest of them, Uncle Alec, was our favorite Wheeler uncle. He was known as "the wild one" as a youth and eventually settled in England. He joined the British army in World War I, rose to the rank of captain, earned the Military Cross and got a piece of shrapnel in his head that occasionally added to his natural lightheartedness.

During one of his round-the-world tours as a young man he invested most of his inheritance in what he thought was a tea plantation in Malaya. It turned out to be a rubber plantation (or perhaps it was the other way around), and to everyone's surprise it flourished so that it provided him with a substantial income for the rest of his life.

He bought Ladbroke, a large manor house near Warwick that eventually became our English base and where several of us and other cousins spent winters hunting the fox. "The Uncle," as we called him, was a charmer and a mad romantic. After one serious affair with a Scandinavian blonde from which Granny bailed him out, he married during the First World War but was soon divorced. Thereafter for twenty years he paid court to most of the beauties of Warwickshire until just before the second war when he married again, this time happily until his death during the war.

Then there was Aunt Tine, the youngest, a tiny, sparrow-like person, who married a British army officer. He was killed during the first war and afterward she decided to move with her four boys to Canada. Though she traveled via Kyneton, she so distrusted American railroads that she shipped all her belongings through the Panama Canal.

I've never been very sure why she made the move in the first place. Perhaps postwar England was too gloomy. Perhaps she wanted her boys brought up in the great open spaces or perhaps she thought she could transplant her household to the colonies and live in Old World luxury in the New World more cheaply. At all events she traveled in the grand manner complete with butler, cook and nanny. But she soon discovered that class-conscious English feudalism did not thrive on New World soil. Soon butler, cook and nanny had caught the democratic infection, struck off for themselves and settled in their own homes around her not as servants but as neighbors—just one big happy family.

This was obviously not what Aunt Tine had planned

and ten years later she moved back to England—presumably to give her boys a little European polish. For a time she and the boys lived at Ladbroke—where I was spending a sabbatical between school and West Point hunting foxes. But then she bought a large and charming country manor where she lived through World War II. By then two of her sons had died, a third had struck it rich in London's City and the fourth, her favorite, had become a Russian language scholar and was appointed professor at the University of Vancouver. So once again she struck camp in England and moved back to Canada, where she died in 1962.

Aunt Ettie was the wit of the family. Physically the exact opposite of Aunt Tine, she was a good feeder, and weighed almost three hundred pounds. A family friend, an explorer, was so impressed by her size and vivacity that he named a volcano after her—"the Burster," as she was called by the family. He also named a glacier after Muzzy—Gaga Glacier. "Gaga" was a childish corruption of Muzzy's real name, Gertrude. Her nieces and nephews always called her Auntie Gaga. Gaga Glacier, Muzzy claimed, was in Australia but as that was one of the few parts of the globe she never visited, she could not prove it.

Aunt Ettie married a Philadelphia surgeon and eventually moved with him to North Carolina, where they built a hospital off in the sticks to take care of the backcountry people of the area.

And finally there was Aunt Bessie, the beauty of the family, who married Uncle Dick and raised a family of four, one of whom—their only son—was killed in World War I. When Uncle Dick died, she too married an Englishman and moved to England where her husband had a fine old manor in the country. During the Blitz in World War II, I was stationed for a time in London and whenever I could I visited Aunt Bessie to get away from the bombs and to enjoy the peaceful luxury of an English country house complete with butler, footmen and fresh eggs.

One evening after Aunt Bessie had left the dinner table, my uncle and I were sipping his port while he held forth on the horrors of the war. He grew more and more agitated and his red face became scarlet as he described the hardships he was being subjected to. I tried to change the subject and complimented him on his excellent port—by then unavailable anywhere in London.

"Humph!" my uncle said with a snort. "Do you know that's my stock for 1948 and I've had to broach it five years early—just because of this damned war!"

THREE

The Troop

Muzzy was twenty-eight and Daddy forty when they married. She was tall, erect and very slim. He was tall too, but stockily built and stooped with wide, sloping shoulders. In contrast to Muzzy's blond hair and mild blue eyes, his hair was dark and his eyes were a deep flashing brown. He wore a full set of whiskers trimmed to a neat goatee and waxed mustaches that could if he wanted give him a rather ferocious appearance, especially as he usually thrust his head forward like a boxer, daring his opponent to take a swing at him.

As a young man Daddy had been a good boxer but he later preferred to spar with his wits, which were just as effective as his fists. His favorite targets were "stuffed shirts" and "jackasses" especially in high places—the higher the places the fiercer his jabs. He had a hot temper and a vivid vocabulary to match it but his outbursts were as brief as they were colorful.

A special victim of his anger was a British army officer called Sam Browne, an utter stranger whom Daddy knew nothing about except that he had invented the Sam Browne belt, a leather contraption with a strap over the right shoulder, which became part of an American officer's uniform.

As a cavalry commander in the National Guard, Daddy often had to lead parades or reviews for eminent visitors. Inevitably as he trotted toward the reviewing stand, with his horse prancing and plunging at the sound of the blaring band, the Sam Browne belt clinging to his sloping shoulder would begin to slip. Just as he brought his saber smartly up to his chin and then down to his knee in salute to the distinguished visitor, the shoulder strap would slide off his shoulder and down his arm, pinning his hand firmly to his side. The music was usually loud enough to drown out the words that streamed from his bearded jaws. But we children, watching anxiously from the sidelines, knew by heart the purple curses he was addressing to Sam Browne.

Muzzy once suggested he fasten the strap up with a safety pin but Daddy dismissed the suggestion as unmilitary. There was nothing he could do, he complained, except shoot that G–d limey Sam Browne.

The Thayers had been brought up in a somewhat less stylish atmosphere than the Wheelers and were not at all impressed by European or English social customs. On the contrary they were robustly American.

They had come from England early in the seventeenth century and settled in Braintree, Massachusetts, whence they spread out in three main directions—Boston, New York and Philadelphia. The Boston contingent, Daddy said, were the brainy ones and distinguished themselves as schoolmasters and scholars. The New York branch were known as the rich Thayers. According to Daddy, there is still a folk saying in upper New York State that "we haven't had such fun since the five Thayers were hanged." Apparently they had all been caught stealing one horse. Daddy boasted that it took a Thayer to pick a horse worth five human necks.

The Philadelphia Thayers liked to consider themselves the athletic Thayers. Their specialty was football. In fact some people say they invented the game. When Daddy was a young man at the University of Pennsylvania, he and some friends wanted to organize a rugby team and sent to England for a book of rules. American football was largely the result of their effort to interpret the book. Years later when Muzzy finally lured Daddy to England, he saw his first game of real rugby and growled that at last he understood what those G–d limeys were trying to say in that rule book twenty years before. But by then it was too late to get American football back on the rugby track.

Daddy was the eldest of five brothers, all of whom went to Penn and were athletes in varying degrees. The second brother, Uncle Johnny, later became a vice-president of the PRR and went down on the *Titanic* while I was still too young to remember him. The third brother, Uncle Sidney, was smaller than Daddy and was more of a cricketer than a football player. Uncle Harry, the fourth brother, was the best football player of them all and was on the first All-America team Walter Camp ever selected. He was also the handsomest of the five brothers and the richest—until the depression, which he blamed exclusively on "that man," Franklin D. Roosevelt.

Once when I was home on leave in the early thirties, I was summoned by the family doctor who told me Uncle Harry was having heart trouble. The doctor warned me sternly that when I went to call on him, I was not to discuss politics or even mention Roosevelt's name as it might give him a stroke.

Uncle Walter, the youngest of the five brothers, was a bachelor and therefore had more time and resources to devote to his nieces and nephews. Naturally he was our favorite. Though less of an athlete than his brothers, he was one of the original old-grad rooters. He seldom missed an athletic event in which a Thayer was playing whether it was an interregional college championship football match in San Francisco or an intramural hockey game at Miss Wright's School in Bryn Mawr.

He usually appeared a little early for the game in order to give the coach the benefit of his advice. Dressed in ear muffs and a long sealskin coat that flapped around his ankles, he trotted up and down the sidelines shouting suggestions and encouragement, stopping occasionally to tell the coach what he was doing wrong.

My father also had one sister but she died before I was born. I still remember Granny Thayer though somewhat dimly. As a child I had difficulty distinguishing the two gray-haired old grannies when they came to call at Kyneton in their carriages. But I knew their coachmen well since I usually stayed out in the stable while the grannies had tea. As a result Granny Thayer was known to me as Martin's Granny and Granny Wheeler was Patrick's.

Martin's Granny's father was a dashing naval officer, George Chapman, a very handsome man judging by his Sully portrait (which looks like every other Sully portrait). He was also something of a hell raiser. His wife, a Markoe, once said she had married George for better or worse but he turned out far worse than she had ever expected. He eventually died as the result of a bet—drinking a bottle of champagne standing on his head.

Daddy, besides playing football and cricket, studied engineering at Penn and eventually became manager of Cramp's Shipyard. But aside from his family and athletics his greatest interest was soldiering, especially the First City Troop.

As a result we grew up with two fanatical loyalties—the Penn football team and the Troop. Since Muzzy's brothers had gone to Harvard, she was originally Harvard-oriented but thanks to Daddy—and the fact that none of her brothers ever was graduated from Harvard

—she switched readily to Penn with all the fervor of a convert. She also became the City Troop's most constant camp follower.

During the football season we lived from Saturday to Saturday in a state of anticipation. When Penn lost, Kyneton was a morgue. When it won, we were intolerably arrogant. Guests who did not share our sympathies were all but driven from the house.

In summer there were always two weeks of Troop camp at Mount Gretna and once a week the rest of the year there was "Troop night." From Daddy we learned every detail of the Troop's glorious history and looked with scorn on similar organizations like Squadron A in New York. To us they were newcomers and rather second-rate at that.

The Troop had been organized in 1774 by a group of Philadelphians to protect the First Continental Congress and, as they put it, "to maintain the rights of the people against the continued oppression of the British Government." Originally called the Light Horse of the City of Philadelphia, it later became the First Troop Philadelphia City Cavalry or more simply the First Troop or to enthusiasts like ourselves the Troop.

The men who established it were chiefly lawyers, bankers or merchants. They provided their own mounts, uniforms and equipment and served without pay except when performing some special chore for the Congress like escorting prominent prisoners or guarding wagon trains of bullion—"conducting cash," they called it. On such occasions they submitted detailed expense accounts directly to the Congress. A typical item from the *Journals of Congress* in Daddy's collection of Troopiana reads:

OCTOBER 17, 1776. To Adam Zantsinger for hire of two wagons and the expenses of an escort of light horse with money from Philadelphia to the camp near New York:
150 60/90 dollars.

In those days Congressional appropriation bills were somewhat simpler than today. Since it was apparently considered unpatriotic to refer to pounds, shillings and pence, the bills were calculated in Spanish dollars, which were worth ninety pence. Hence the 60/90ths.

One of our proudest boasts was that the first captain of the Troop, Abraham Markoe, was our great-great-grandfather. Markoe originally came from the Danish West Indies where he had many relatives and much property. When the Danish government, of which he was a subject, declared itself neutral in the Revolutionary War, Markoe found it expedient to resign the captaincy to protect his relatives and property—a fact that we generally skipped over lightly.

Aside from the Troop's being the first military unit of the Revolutionary government, its flag, designed by Markoe, was the first to bear thirteen stripes representing the thirteen colonies—which in our eyes made Betsy Ross's Stars and Stripes a downright plagiarism.

Because of their unique status as self-supporting volunteers, the Troopers assumed the privilege of going home whenever there was nothing serious to be done like fighting a battle or conducting cash. In those days wars were usually neatly divided into campaigns with rest periods in between, especially when the weather was bad. The Revolution was no exception, and whenever General Washington called time out for rest or winter bivouac, the Troopers went home to attend to their businesses. One of them in fact was ordered home in the middle of a campaign to "manufacture such quantities of soapp and candelles" as were needed by the army. However, he evidently was enjoying the campaign for he refused to go home to make the "soapp and candelles."

To us children hearing Daddy tell it, the arrangement seemed perfectly natural. If the Penn football team could take time out in the middle of a game, why not the Troop in the middle of a war?

On active service the Troop usually served as personal bodyguard to General Washington. He obviously recognized the importance of the Troopers' business affairs and raised no objections when they went home. In 1775, when he was on his way to take command of the army in Massachusetts, the Troop escorted him as far as New York where he dismissed them, stating that he did not wish "the gentlemen of the troop to be longer absent from Philadelphia." War might be hell but business was business.

Daddy and his children were infuriated when in 1911 Charles Francis Adams, the Boston historian, wrote that "the detailed history of the Troop . . . forcibly illustrates the quite disorganized and wholly unreliable character of the mounted forces attached to Washington's army at the time."

"Unreliable indeed!" Daddy said angrily. "And what the hell were the Adamses doing when the Troop was formed? Making speeches!" We children nodded in vehement agreement.

In rebuttal to Adams, Daddy cited the Troop's services in the Revolution, not only acting as bodyguard to the Commander in Chief when he was in the Philadelphia area but also providing scouts, raiding parties and pickets. It formed the rear guard during Washington's retreat across the Delaware and the vanguard during the subsequent recrossing when he captured Trenton from the Hessians. It was also with him during the disheartening defeat inflicted by Lord Howe at the Brandywine. Afterward when Washington's regulars went into winter quarters at Valley Forge, the Troopers found quarters in neighboring villages and remained ready for any special duty the Commander in Chief might request.

Compared to the Troopers, as Daddy frequently pointed out, a great many "gentlemen" not only in Philadelphia but in New York and Boston as well were considerably less than loyal to the Revolution. Some were outspoken Tories. Others refused to take the oath of allegiance to the Revolutionary authorities. While the Troopers, for example, lived in self-imposed exile around Valley Forge, other less patriotic gentlemen were having a fine time in Philadelphia with the British occupiers under Lord Howe. Their disloyalty was not quickly forgotten.

I once asked Daddy why the ———s, a prominent

Philadelphia family, were often excluded from city social activities.

"Son," I recall his replying tartly, "don't you know that the ——s gave a ball for Lord Howe after the battle of Brandywine?"

Some Philadelphians claim my memory is faulty and the charge apocryphal. However, the minutes of the Supreme Executive (Revolutionary) Council for 1777 contain the notation that one of the most outspoken opponents of the Revolutionary government was "Benja. —— Esq'r." The Council therefore requested "an officer and six gentlemen of the Philadelphia Light Horse to escort . . . Benja. —— Esq'r. as prisoner in Fredericksburg, Virginia."

Whether —— got out of jail in time to give the alleged ball for Lord Howe is not recorded but Troopers like Daddy still remembered his lack of Revolutionary ardor a hundred and fifty years later.

During the Civil War, too, the Troop was one of the first to volunteer for service—for three months—after which the Troopers as usual returned to their law offices and banks. But when Lee invaded Pennsylvania, they rejoined the colors at once and helped drive him out of Pennsylvania at Gettysburg.

Daddy was elected to the Troop in 1893. It was a slow time for soldiers, and until the outbreak of the Spanish-American War five years later, he served as a private. He was in Russia selling ships to the Czar's government when hostilities broke out. He hurried home, joined the Troop, and was promptly promoted to corporal.

After endless delays, which Daddy attributed to the incompetence of the politicians and generals in Harrisburg and Washington, the Troop was finally mustered into the federal service, re-equipped with "modern" weapons and sent off, horses and all, to Puerto Rico where they landed at the beginning of August in 1898, or rather, their ship ran aground. They finally managed to get themselves and their horses ashore in lighters and hurried forward to the front, which they reached on August 13th. There they received orders to storm a Spanish fort with a mounted charge after a preliminary artillery bombardment. Sober tacticians might have pointed out that cavalry charges against forts had gone out of fashion around the time of the siege of Troy but it was all in keeping with the spirit of the war with Spain and the troopers were jubilant.

All their training in the Troop had been pointed toward the supreme maneuver—the cavalry charge. Every year at the end of two long weeks of drilling, they had staged a mock charge across the plain at Mount Gretna, usually ending with runaway horses streaking across the parade ground, which lay strewn with the bodies of unhorsed rookies writhing in varying degrees of disability.

Now at last they were to charge in earnest with real rifles cracking at them and live bullets whistling past them. Daddy loved to describe it all in detail. As they stood by their mounts they checked their equipment, inspected the girths of their saddles, and adjusted their stirrups. Several of them drew their sabers and flourished them in the air for a final rehearsal of the thrusts and parries they had practiced every Monday night for years at the Troop Armory on 21st Street. Others patted their horses' necks and whispered into their ears brave words of encouragement designed to maintain their own morale as much as the animals'.

At their head Captain Groome fidgeted in his saddle waiting for the preliminary bombardment and cursing the artillery's slowness. Behind him the Troop trumpeter fingered his bugle nervously, wetting his lips from time to time and humming to himself the notes of that most glorious of all bugle calls, "Charge!"

Then from beyond them they heard the pounding of galloping hoofs as a courier rode up, drew rein in front of the captain and saluted.

The war, he announced, was over.

So abandoning their horses they all went home to Philadelphia. There they were cheered as heroes as they paraded up Broad Street on horses borrowed from the city police. Daddy never forgave the artillery for its slowness with that bombardment.

In 1916 when Wilson sent General Pershing to catch Pancho Villa in Mexico, the Troop was mobilized again and sent to the border. Daddy was married by now so Muzzy, quite naturally, packed her sidesaddle in an enormous box and, taking my older brother George with her, reported for camp-following duty in El Paso. To the Troopers' intense indignation, Pershing left them behind to guard the boundary while he set off after Villa. For months they patrolled across the hot desert accompanied by Muzzy elegantly riding in her sidesaddle with brother George less elegantly following behind bareback on a donkey, his bare feet dragging in the sand. Eventually Pershing returned from his chase empty-handed. "Naturally," the Troopers said contemptuously with a frustrated shrug of their shoulders.

In 1917 when the United States finally entered the First World War, Daddy was captain of the Troop, which was mobilized at once. Many of its members had accepted officers' commissions in newly formed army units and, to replace them and bring the Troop to war strength, Daddy had to recruit a large number of young men. He immediately suspended the rules for electing new members from among the circle of friends of existing members and sought volunteers from wherever he could find them. The resulting "volunteer troop" was, I think, one of Daddy's proudest accomplishments for it represented not simply the hard-drinking, hard-riding gentlemen of Philadelphia society but men from every sort of background.

However, Daddy's satisfaction was short-lived. By then the fighting on the Western Front had degenerated into a bloody trench war of foot soldiers. The generals in Europe, mesmerized by their own murderous creation, decided there was no room for cavalry in the trenches. Daddy thought otherwise and in often caustic messages to the Governor of the State, to the General Staff in Washington and even to Newton Baker, the Secretary of War, he expounded the view that only cavalry could break the stalemate. But the authorities were not accustomed to taking advice from a National Guard captain.

Meantime the Troop had been sent for training to

Augusta, Georgia, and Muzzy once again packed her sidesaddle and, gathering such children as were available from school, hastened after it. There she rented a summer house where we shivered throughout the winter (the coldest in Georgia's history) while she dispensed aid and comfort to the homesick Troopers. The only important event of that era, I recall, was when Avis sat on an oilstove, which left a permanent brand on her backside.

Then suddenly orders came from Washington to transform the Troop into a trench-mortar company. Even its name and the guidon it had carried for nearly a hundred and fifty years were ordered to be discarded.

At retreat on the evening of its last day as a troop of cavalry all of us went to the camp. As Daddy stood grim and erect at the head of the Troop street and the Troop trumpeter shakily sounded "Retreat," the old guidon with the legendary "F.T.P.C.C." was furled for the last time. It was the only time I ever saw tears stream down Daddy's cheeks into his gray beard.

To make matters worse, when the Troop was finally sent overseas the War Department decided that its cantankerous captain, then approaching sixty, was too old to lead a trench-mortar company in action. So Daddy was ordered to Oklahoma to learn to be an artillery officer. There he made life miserable for his instructors, most of them at least a generation younger than he. When a young West Point lieutenant wound up a lecture by asking for questions, Daddy rose in wrath and told the young whippersnapper that he hadn't understood one G–d word he had said.

Shortly afterward when Averell Harriman asked Daddy to run his shipyard, then making Liberty ships, the War Department urged him to accept. Reluctantly Daddy agreed.

Muzzy and I, still faithful camp followers, were living at the time in a desolate little Oklahoma town called Lawton. We had a room in a boarding house and ate at a drugstore counter. It was not at all like life at Kyneton. But we considered it our contribution to the war effort. We also saved our sugar and gave it to Daddy and his friends.

Muzzy undertook to do our wash, borrowed a laundry tub from the landlady and went to work. A little while later as Muzzy was struggling with our underwear, the landlady looked in and watched her for a minute or two. Then she said with a smile, "Dearie, I'd like to bet you never did a piece of laundry before in your life." Muzzy blushed scarlet but, unable to deny the charge, stood silent while the landlady took over.

So when Daddy finally decided his fighting career was over and it was time to go home, we were secretly delighted to return to the more familiar atmosphere of the Main Line.

And then Muzzy suddenly had an inspiration: why not motor back to Philadelphia? Remembering his experiences with the Wedding Present, Daddy was skeptical but eventually he gave in and bought a Ford from a local dealer.

In those days tourism was not well developed in Oklahoma but there was a road called the Ozark Trail that led eastward so we set off down the trail, Daddy at the wheel. It wound across the desert, very occasionally passing through an Indian village or a small town. Sometimes the town had a gas station and on rare occasions even a garage but mostly there was only a bar and a row of hitching posts.

Our first day's progress was cut short after a couple of hours and about forty miles when Daddy discovered the man who had sold him the car had failed to include oil for the motor in the deal. There was some purple fulmination when Daddy unearthed this fact. Determined not to return to Lawton, of which we all three had had enough, we persuaded a passing truck to tow us to the next town, ten miles to the east. It was a dusty ride behind the truck since the Ozark Trail was not, of course, tarred.

It took a day or two to repair the burned-out engine but then we set off again. It was a hot sunny day and we were all eager to get on—except for the car. However, Daddy kept it going for several hours and almost a hundred miles when something went wrong again. Once more we got a passing truck to tow us to the next town and since whatever was wrong was not too serious we were off again next day on the third lap.

For a while it seemed our troubles were over. The car purred along happily. Daddy whistled "There's a long, long trail" and Muzzy enjoyed the view—thinking, no doubt, how pleasant it would be to sink back into Kyneton life complete with butler, maids and laundresses.

But then Daddy's vigilance must have relaxed for we

hit a bump as we whizzed along at nearly thirty miles an hour. There was a grinding sound in the rear and the car stopped. Daddy silently opened the door, got out and looked at the rear axle. Even I could see it was broken in two. Daddy's face was black as he put his hands on his hips, thrust his bearded chin forward and strode out into the desert, staring unseeing at the shimmering wasteland. Muzzy bit her lower lip and looked as though she were about to burst into tears. I was more terrified than I had ever been in my life—not because Daddy was angry. That happened regularly. It was his silence that distressed me. If only a string of curses would explode from him, I knew he would soon be all right. But for once his anger was more than his versatile vocabulary could cope with.

Somehow we got to the next town, sold the car and settled back in the drawing room of a Pullman bound for the East Coast. Both Muzzy and Daddy seemed relieved. We had been traveling almost a week and had covered something less than three hundred miles. Touring by car might be the thing of the future, but for Daddy it was a thing of the past. Ever since his brother-in-law had given him the Wedding Present, he had been at war with the internal-combustion engine and though he continued fighting gallantly the odds against him were hopeless.

Back home at Kyneton we continued the war effort by knitting socks and sweaters for the soldiers. I became a fairly proficient knitter but to my shame I always had to call for help when it came to turning the Kitchener toe, as it was called for some odd reason. Muzzy even organized a class of ladies to knit under the supervision of our two German nurses. While the ladies knit for their relatives on our side of the trenches, the nurses knit for their relatives on the other side. War was like that in those days—at least at Kyneton.

(It was different in the Second World War. There was less knitting but Muzzy found other ways to serve. Years later I discovered among her papers a Certificate of Excellence from the War Department inscribed to Muzzy for her work in the Service Men's Snack Bar of the Church of the Good Shepherd.)

As soon as the First World War ended, Daddy was appointed a colonel of the National Guard and, still unmoved by Newton Baker's views on cavalry, began getting his cavalry regiment ready for the next war. For two weeks each summer he took the regiment to summer camp and I always went along as his orderly. While Daddy spent the day riding about the drill fields, the picket lines and the tent camp, lacerating the unfortunates who fell off their horses or failed to clean the insides of their tents or the bellies of their mounts, I sneaked away with the map-making detail of the Headquarters Troop. I was already determined to be a soldier when I grew up and I had read that both Washington and Napoleon had started out as surveyors.

Though I loved camp, I dreaded the last night of each year's training. For then, knowing that next day they would be immune to K.P. and the other punishments Daddy meted out to miscreants, the soldiers always got drunk and sometimes even disorderly. The results were apt to be disagreeable. Once Daddy awoke from sleep on the last night and heard the riotous cavalrymen whooping it up down the line. Clad in a nightshirt, he called out the guard and strode angrily down to where the noise came from. Aware that his authority would go with the dawn, Daddy ordered the staggering drinkers to pick up a large heavy telegraph pole and tote it up and down the Troop street until reveille. The victims unfortunately were my friends from the mapping squad, and when I went to say goodbye to them next day, I was deeply hurt by their coolness to the colonel's son.

Despite his harsh discipline Daddy was worshiped by his men and even after he died I was welcomed back to Mount Gretna every year as orderly to his successors, either the colonel of the regiment or the captain of the reorganized First City Troop. However, it was never quite the same. Daddy's military career had been long and frustrating—thirty years without ever seeing action. But it had always been exciting, especially when we passed in review before the Governor at the gallop. I rode just behind Daddy, who cursed steadily as runaway Troopers streaked across the plain and behind us pounded the full regiment of cavalry.

After World War II, when the horse cavalry was finally abolished by an infantryman, Dwight Eisenhower, the Troop was issued armored cars instead of horses. Today when it escorts distinguished visitors, it has to borrow horses from the Park Guards. But it still wears its resplendent full-dress uniform with its blue coat, white breeches, high black boots and a black helmet surmounted by a bearskin plume.

The uniform was originally modeled after the European uniforms of the Revolutionary period and when a Britisher once commented on its similarity to that of the British Horse Guards, Daddy replied tartly but inaccurately, "Only the tails—it's all we ever saw of the British."

Not that Daddy was anti-British. He must have found Granny Wheeler's anglophilia a bit ridiculous, for his own tastes ran definitely to the blunter American manner. But he admired the British military tradition and its crack cavalry regiments.

Once in London he was wandering aimlessly through the West End when he came upon the barracks of one of the Guards regiments. He marched up to the sentry, asked to see the Officer of the Guard and explained that he was a member of the Philadelphia City Troop. The guardsman, delighted by his lack of ceremony, invited him to the officer's mess, where the Revolutionary campaigns and particularly the Battle of the Brandywine were refought under more convivial circumstances than the original contests.

A fervent democrat and a black Republican, Daddy had little use for titles political, military or hereditary. He despised politicians, found generals basically backward and titled Europeans a touch absurd. When the King of the Belgians once gave him a medal for commanding his escort on a visit to Philadelphia, Daddy pointed out that the King had given the same medal to the porter on the Pullman that had brought him to town.

On another occasion before World War I, a Russian naval detachment came to Philadelphia to take delivery of a battleship Cramps had built for them. Daddy, who was a great admirer of the Russians, invited the entire crew out to Kyneton for a buffet lunch. Twenty years later I was traveling through Russia and in Baku struck up a conversation with an ancient bootblack who had once been in the Czarist navy. He said he had once visited my hometown of Philadelphia to pick up a battleship. And then to my utter amazement he told me about that buffet lunch down to the last detail, including the old oak tree under which the tables were set up. "It was the only time in all my years at sea that the men were invited along with the officers," he commented.

Daddy's attitude toward politicians was more or less typical of those Philadelphians who had moved out of the city to the Main Line, abandoning it to the ward bosses who swindled it for sixty years until they were thrown out by the reformers in the forties.

While he was a great believer in public service and brought up both my brother and me to enter government, he was convinced that politics was not a service but a racket. Politicians he considered either unscrupulous thrusters trying to get their feet into the public trough or fools, or both. When a cousin of ours entered politics and made a name for himself in Washington, Daddy simply shrugged his shoulders. "Your cousin," he explained to us, "cheated as a boy at the deLancey School."

FOUR

Mechanized

IT TOOK Daddy several years to recover from the motor trip in Oklahoma. Though by now nearly all our friends and neighbors were motorized, Daddy still had grave doubts about the role of the car in modern society. Fiercely loyal to his *obiter dictum* that the car was a passing fad, we children scorned the horseless carriage and when our neighbors boasted of having cars with twenty or thirty horsepower we laughed them out of the house. Imagine a tin contraption like that being equal to forty horses like Daddy's mount Harry!

And when the Borax Twenty-Mule Team once went by on the Gulph Road we cheered wildly, and contemptuously dared our car-owning friends to match their automobiles with Borax's twenty mules. Even they seemed dubious that day.

But then one hot July evening (July 10th to be exact,

for it was Muzzy's birthday) there was an odd roar on the front drive and we rushed out just in time to see Daddy charging up driving a Model T Ford, his eyes flashing, his beard thrust forward and his hands holding the wheel as though he had a wild monster by the throat. He parked the car in front of the door and then with a grand gesture presented it to Muzzy.

Muzzy was delighted but our reactions were mixed. As the only family in the neighborhood to have remained faithful to the horse, we were reluctant now suddenly to turn against him and become the Johnny-come-latelies of the horseless age. Besides, the clatter it made was terrifying. In those days all cars made a dreadful racket but no one could get as much noise out of one as Daddy.

But when we finally became used to the clatter, we were thrilled with the sensation of whizzing down the drive and along Spring Mill Road at twenty-five miles an hour. Even we had to admit that Daddy's horse Harry couldn't gallop that fast.

Despite Muzzy's delight—she was always fascinated by new gadgets—Daddy was still skeptical and never really came to terms with the internal-combustion engine. The Ford reciprocated his animosity. Whenever he put his powerful shoulder to the crank, you could almost see its back go up like a fractious horse. Whether Daddy pulled the little ring that choked the engine or didn't, the car would just cough, shiver a little and remain silent. Daddy never remained silent. A stream of cuss words would pour from him as he cranked and pulled the choke. Then pausing, hands on hips, he would glower furiously at the brass radiator and walk around the car to rearrange the gas and spark levers under the steering wheel. Then he would crank again and likely as not the car would emit a terrifying backfire and sullenly subside.

It usually took about ten minutes before the Ford knew it had gone far enough riling Daddy and then with a joyful crash of thunder the engine would take hold, the whole body shaking with enthusiasm. Daddy would run around the car to adjust the levers again but we children would leap back just in case the whole contraption should suddenly explode.

When we acquired the Ford, there was no corresponding reduction of horses in the stable. You could never be sure when the car fad would die out and Daddy was not going to be left stranded in the post-automobile age with a broken-down Ford and an empty stable.

For much the same reason, there was no question of hiring a chauffeur as some of our richer neighbors had—a man schooled to the mysteries of the engine. On the contrary John Nagle, the coachman, could be taught to drive and who better to teach him than Daddy?

John had been born in County Killarney and one of his first jobs as a young immigrant had been as stableboy at my grandmother's where he had married the head coachman's sister Lizzy. When Muzzy and Daddy got married, John and Lizzy joined them as cook and coachman.

Muzzy was never quite sure whether Lizzy would

work out as a cook. She was still uncertain several decades later when she came to visit me in Berlin where I was a vice-consul. She was telling me the news from home when she abruptly switched the subject and asked, obviously conscious that as a resident of Europe I was already a connoisseur of cooking, whether I thought Lizzy had the makings of a good cook. "Do you think she can be trained?" Muzzy asked.

I said, "But, Muzzy, how long has she been cooking?"

Muzzy looked vague as she tried to make the mental calculation. Then suddenly her eyes brightened. "But of course I know, it'll be fifty years next spring. And you must be home for the anniversary. We're giving her a silver platter." Lizzy and John eventually retired after seventy-one years with the family.

But to return to the Ford, until Daddy produced it John had never seen inside the hood of a motorcar. He listened perplexed and worried as Daddy with the air of an expert talking to a child explained first how to start the car. Then Daddy demonstrated for ten minutes or so till he got it going. Finally he switched off the engine and suggested John try. John cautiously adjusted the levers of the steering wheel, forgot the choke, spun the crank and the car began to hum quietly. Daddy smiled superciliously. Typical of an ignorant Irishman's beginner's luck, he said later.

Then he clambered up behind the wheel and John, trembling with fright, sat gingerly beside him, his hand on the unclosed door ready to jump if necessary. Daddy demonstrated the three foot pedals: the gear pedal, which you pushed down all the way for low and then slowly let out to put the car in high, the reverse pedal in the middle and finally the brake pedal.

Then as we children watched, they set off down the back drive. The expression on John's face was one of abject terror. Lizzy, standing by the kitchen door as they roared by, shook her head and wiped her sweating hands on her apron. It was the last she would ever see of her husband, she probably thought, and mumbled a prayer to Saint Christopher.

A few minutes later there was a roaring sound on the front drive as the Ford charged up the hill, Daddy tense at the wheel. Around they sped again, down the back drive and up the front, John still wide-eyed, his mouth half open, as Daddy demonstrated the fine art of driving.

Then suddenly the car sped around again and this time to our amazement John was huddled over the wheel jerking it spasmodically from side to side.

John was now officially chauffeur as well as coachman. I stress the word "officially" for never in the scores of years he drove did he make the psychological transfer from the horse to the engine. Whenever he drove downhill, for example, he leaned back and tugged on the steering wheel lest the front wheels stumble. Going uphill, he rocked back and forth and chirruped to the engine as though he were encouraging a tired team up a steep grade. Only when it was about to stall would he remember to give it more gas.

But worst of all was his shying. If a bit of paper or a

bird suddenly fluttered in the ditch, John would jerk the wheel and shy halfway across the road, just as though he were driving a skittish mare.

Even when he washed the car, he would sponge it with exactly the same circular motion he used with a currycomb and brush, hissing through his teeth like every experienced groom to keep the dust from the car's hide out of his mouth.

Nevertheless, to Daddy's ill-concealed annoyance and envy, he did somehow "have a way" with the Ford as he did with the most troublesome horse. And often when Daddy had given up trying to crank the car, John would shuffle up diffidently and with a few twists of the wrist have the car purring like a cat.

And then, of course, it was Muzzy's turn to learn. In those days ladies did not generally drive cars but Muzzy was determined from the first that she was going to conquer the new invention just as she conquered the others that were to follow—the radio, the oil furnace, the TV and finally, in a sense, the Sputnik itself. She knew hardly more than John Nagle about the inner workings of the car and it was more of a moral conquest than an intellectual or scientific one. The aim was to make the contraption take you where you wanted no matter whether it could or would. It was like a stubborn lead horse in the tandem team, which had to be wrestled with and shown who was master.

Because Daddy was away all day, John was elected as Muzzy's teacher. They understood each other perfectly, and since their attitudes toward the car were similar, the lessons were fairly successful. At first Muzzy was inclined to acquire John's habits of clucking, swaying and tugging back on the wheel going downhill and even shying occasionally, but by the time she was seventy, she had overcome these defects only to acquire others.

Muzzy had hardly made two laps around the drive when she announced she knew how to drive. To prove it she decided to drive the whole family down to Granny's house, Pembroke, for tea. We all piled in, the four older children in back, myself on John's knee in front and my youngest sister, Avis, propped between Muzzy and John. It was a full load and a happy one for we were all blissfully confident of Muzzy's new accomplishment.

But our confidence was short-lived. We dashed down the back way along the bumpy unsurfaced Gulph Road at great speed (Muzzy had not yet learned about broken springs) and we were soon making our approach to the narrow gate in the high stone wall around Pembroke. Unfortunately Uncle Charlie, driving a luxurious Stutz and dressed in a duster and motoring cap, was approaching from inside the gate for a take-off. As Muzzy swung the car energetically at the gate as though it were a jump, she caught sight of Uncle Charlie's car charging at her. Her first instinct was to jerk back on the steering wheel. When the car didn't slow, she swerved off along the strip of grass between the wall and the ditch. Uncle Charlie swerved too—into the gatepost. We all screeched, terrified. John yelped like a jackal and tried to reach for the brake but I on his lap and Avis beside him were in the way, so instead he turned off the ignition.

But the car kept rolling. Ahead was a telegraph pole and the gap between it and the wall was clearly less than the width of the Model T. As the car coasted to a halt, the two front fenders crumpled between the pole and the stone wall.

There was a dead silence and then Muzzy, looking around, saw her brother striding angrily toward her. She bit her lip and, turning to John, exploded with her most vehement curse: "Thundering guns, John! What ever got into this car?"

John had soon pounded out the tin fenders of the Ford but Uncle Charlie's Stutz had to be towed to the carriage makers' in Bryn Mawr. The wall was rebuilt—just as narrow and blind as before—and eventually relations between Muzzy and Uncle Charlie were back to normal. Though she never entirely regained the confidence of her children, she continued to drive us about with verve and at least self-confidence.

Nevertheless she was too fond of the horse not to recognize the disadvantages of the car. There was all that cranking business to get the car started—not just the flick of a whip on a horse's back. And then you had to get gasoline for it—a complicated problem in those days. To get hay and oats for the horses was no problem. All you did was call the feed store and they would send out a wagonload. But gasoline filling stations were in many places still unheard of and gasoline distributors were rare. Finally, she installed a tank and a pump in the stable.

But she had to admit there were advantages. When she

stopped somewhere, she didn't have to have a groom hold the car or tie it to a hitching post. It just stayed where it was. Or so she thought until one day when she had parked the car at the front door at the top of the drive.

When she came back to get it, the car was gone. She sent word through Augustus to ask John what he meant by taking away the car. A message came back that John hadn't touched the car. Impatiently Muzzy shrugged her shoulders but kept her temper. To no one in particular she muttered, "Oh dear! What could John be thinking about?" Then she told Augustus to ask John to find the car. She needed it at once. John searched the stable, the drive, even looked up and down Spring Mill Road lest the car had gone out by itself. But there was no car in sight.

Muzzy was beside herself with impatience at John. "Thundering guns! How could he lose the Ford?" she muttered as she abandoned her planned excursion and went upstairs to change from her motoring clothes.

Next morning Mullen, the gardener, an archenemy of John's, announced he had solved the mystery of the disappearing Ford. He pointed to a large Japanese weeping cherry tree down near the foot of the drive. Sullenly John went down to the tree and there, hidden under its long caressing branches, was the Ford. Thenceforth Muzzy tried to remember to put on the brake when she left the car on a hill. She was not always successful. However, after the cherry-tree episode we knew where to look when the Ford vanished.

Except for ceremonial occasions, Muzzy preferred to drive the car herself just as she had always preferred to drive carriages. But at weddings and similar events she bowed to convention and, dressed in her finest clothes, she sat elegantly in the back of the car, a little terrified, while John drove. I think these were the happiest events in John's life. For one thing it gave him an excuse to wear his best uniform and his shiniest cap. But more than that it gave him a chance to get together with his colleagues "in the back" while the gentry were sipping champagne "in the front."

Not all the chauffeurs were trained mechanics. The majority were ex-coachmen like John, and while they waited for their employers they gossiped and reminisced about the good old days and boasted about the horses and carriages they had once driven. And then there was the final excitement as the guests began to leave. For it was a matter of honor to have your car at the head of the line at the front door when your employer made his departure. The jockeying and maneuvering that went on among the chauffeurs to be first off was as exciting to them as it was to riders at the starting gate in a steeplechase.

Occasionally John even drove in town but that was a thrill few of us relished. He didn't mind Philadelphia's narrow streets—had he not often driven carriages through them? It was the trolley cars that unhinged him. They were so big and determined-looking when they charged up Chestnut Street, their clanging bells imperiously summoning all comers to get out of the way, that John always gave them a wide berth. In fact his usual reaction when he saw one of the monsters coming was to drive up on the sidewalk and wait for it to go past.

Fortunately as small children we seldom went to town with John except to go to the dentist, Dr. Woodward. Dr. Woodward was, it seemed to me, in his nineties when I first visited him. His hands shook and so did his knees, but Muzzy had gone to him since she was a child and in such matters she was a traditionalist.

Dr. Woodward's assistant was called Miss Murray. Her chief function was to regulate the speed on the mechanical drill while Dr. Woodward concentrated as best as he could on trying to guide it into cavities. He was not always successful.

As soon as we were in the chair, still shaking from our drive with John, Dr. Woodward reached for the drill, of which he was very proud. I suspect it was one of the first invented. Then he forced open our mouths and, breathing down our throats. let out his war cry: "First speed to the right, Miss Murray!" I can't recall his ever using anything but the first speed and it was always to the right. I shudder to think what would have happened if he had ever called for a speed to the left.

Our only consolation for dentist trips was that we could go to Whitman's for an ice-cream soda when it was all over. Considering that several of us, including Muzzy, lost our natural teeth at a relatively early age, I'm not sure that Whitman's was adequate compensation for Dr. Woodward's first speed to the right.

FIVE

Kyneton

EVEN BEFORE they were married, Muzzy and Daddy scoured the countryside on horseback looking for a site for their future home. They finally chose a windy, barren hill in Villa Nova about three miles west of Bryn Mawr. It was surrounded by several large farms, many of them belonging to cousins and friends. We children, eying the hundreds of acres our neighbors owned, sometimes felt we were living in a slum on a mere fourteen acres but Muzzy and Daddy found it more than enough. And eventually when Kyneton was sold, it was almost the only place in the neighborhood of more than two or three acres, our neighbors' farms having long since been gobbled up by developers and converted into rabbit warrens of suburbia.

Except for an ancient oak that still stands and two

large chestnuts that died in the chestnut blight, the hill was treeless. So while the house was being built, Muzzy and Daddy studded it with lime trees, beeches, fruit trees and dogwood. And along the fence lines they assiduously planted bushes of honeysuckle.

Fifty years later one of Muzzy's last chores before she was grounded was to climb the trees she had planted and prune them back to prevent them from growing in through the windows. As for the honeysuckle, it had become the scourge of the countryside. When a neighbor reproached Muzzy for planting it in the first place, she smiled wistfully.

"It was silly of me." she admitted, adding with a sly twinkle, "but then we all did it in those days, didn't we?"

The house itself was large and roomy to accommodate the family Muzzy promised herself, but it was not big enough and had to be enlarged a few years later. Whoever designed it did not share modern architects' passion for compactness. There was enough waste space in halls and odd corners to provide room for a second house. The front hall ran the width of the house and served no useful purpose except as an assembly area or for guests who could not say goodbye promptly to linger in exchanging last-minute endearments. Off it were two more halls, one leading to "the back" and the other to the drawing room. Besides the large dining room there was a third room filled with bookshelves, which anyone else would have called a library but which Muzzy named "the schoolroom," probably because English houses always had schoolrooms (and libraries too).

Upstairs was another series of useless halls, a day nursery, a night nursery, a morning room where Muzzy did her desk chores, Daddy's dressing room and a big master bedroom with a four-poster, a fireplace, a prie-dieu for Muzzy and a dressing table where, I remember, she sat getting dressed for dinner while her maid brushed her long blond hair.

Muzzy was a fanatic about fresh air and off the master bedroom she built a sleeping porch. It was held up by two slender posts that were forever rotting. When we protested that the porch was about to fall down, Muzzy unfailingly procrastinated, explaining that the bank wouldn't let her have the money to repair it. The porch was filled with canvas army cots on which all of us slept under piles of blankets Muzzy got at the Army & Navy Stores. They were heavy and scratchy. The hard cots and the scratchy blankets were supposed to make us tough. Whether they did or not, they greatly increased our appreciation of beds and sheets when we were allowed to sleep in them.

At first the porch was uncovered. Roofs, Muzzy explained, kept out the fresh air. So when it rained, we woke up drenched and sleepily went indoors to our otherwise useless beds. When it snowed, we burrowed lower in the blankets and woke next morning with inches of snow covering us.

Later on Muzzy relented and had a canvas cover stretched over the porch. But like the posts that held it up the canvas quickly rotted and ripped, so that the rain and snow did not fall evenly upon us but were channeled in roaring torrents through the holes. Only after a spark from the chimney burned up the canvas roof did Muzzy finally get around to buying a new one.

Directly above the master bedroom was another large room known as the Freezer, later modernized by the grandchildren to the Deep Freeze, so called because no matter how much the furnace was stoked no whiff of warm air ever reached it. It was furnished with half a dozen beds always made up and ready for stray guests. There was also a spare room but it was reserved for formal visits of aunts, uncles or older cousins. The spare room contained a secret drawer, where Muzzy kept a cache of toys and other presents for emergency use when one of us was ill or otherwise needed morale-building. Later on I used it to house my zebra finches until the oil-furnace calamity.

A narrow steep set of steps between the master bedroom and the morning room opened through a trap door in the Freezer, a precaution in case anyone was trapped in the distant dormitory by fire. But Muzzy, who loved to live dangerously, obviously thought her guests must also like to. So she stacked the steps with household hardware: open boxes of nails and tacks, hammers and saws, extra light bulbs and other sharp implements designed to cut to ribbons anyone who dared use the emergency fire escape. Fortunately there never was a fire at Kyneton aside from the sleeping-porch roof and an occasional chimney.

Why there wasn't a fire mystified the insurance agents for years until they concluded Muzzy lived under some special form of divine protection. Kyneton's electric system, installed at the turn of the century, was itself so fragile that it could have set fire to a stone wall, let alone the tinderbox Kyneton quickly became. Besides when the first fuse blew, Muzzy discovered the trick of shorting the fuses with pennies. Soon the fuse box was fully equipped with pennies and to Muzzy's delight she was never again bothered by a burned-out fuse.

Sixty years later a crew of lighting electricians came to set up a television interview with my brother-in-law at Kyneton. They took one look at the wiring and whistled. Then they opened the fuse box, paled and slammed it shut before it blew up in their faces. In the end they laid a cable of their own to the nearest electric substation half a mile down the road.

The location of the Freezer on the third floor directly over Muzzy's bedroom occasionally led to confusion. When Bobby, a young beau of the girls', came back to spend the night after a gay party, he was apparently so befuddled that he couldn't count. When he got to the second floor, he tottered to the front room and climbed into the first bed he came to. Fortunately Muzzy was sleeping on the porch. When she came in the next morning, she was mildly surprised to find a young man sleeping soundly in her bed. It was the last time Bobby spent the night at Kyneton for years.

When it came to actually building the house, some say the contractor was drunk. Others claim a friend sold

Daddy some green lumber. But whatever the cause, the chief structural characteristic of Kyneton was its permeability. Not a window or a door fitted its frame. In summer it was cool and breezy. But in winter the winds seeped through every opening, keeping the inside temperature just above freezing.

The big mahogany front door was the chief offender despite its heavy brass weather stripping. For it not only let the wind through but kept up a low dismal moan all winter, which rose to a terrifying shriek when the north wind blew. But it served one useful purpose, for when it shrieked it was a signal for us to man the north windows, which always blew open in a storm. So when we heard the signal, we fanned out quickly over the house to shut the windows while the servants came with mops to sop up the water and snow.

There was one advantage in the weak fastenings. Every night we solemnly went through the ritual of locking up, which meant turning the big lock in the front door. Thereafter, late-comers or house guests we had forgotten had only to go around to the nearest French window and walk in.

The openness of Kyneton also seemed to have a favorable psychological effect on potential burglars, who apparently assumed that there could scarcely be much worth-while loot in the big unlocked house on the hill. Whenever there was a rash of burglaries in the neighborhood, Kyneton was so ostentatiously ignored that Muzzy got quite offended.

Friends of Muzzy's say that when the house was

finally finished, she had visions of furnishing it exquisitely in the style of a little French château. If true, there was no evidence of it by the time I came along. Muzzy managed somehow to cope with the stuffed antelope heads and elephant feet that her trophy-happy brothers used to send her from Africa or India.

She even found a use for the moosehead Uncle Charlie shot in Alaska. She used its right nostril to hide the key of the liquor closet in. Just from whom it was hidden was never clear, for over the years every child, guest and servant had rummaged about the nostril and found the key. Eventually the nostril began to come apart and sag dolefully, so Muzzy sent for a taxidermist to repair the shredded nose. When he had sewn it up, he suggested caustically that Muzzy find a better hiding place for the key to the liquor closet.

"Another place for the key?" Muzzy said, frowning as she considered this revolutionary suggestion.

"Dear me. . . . But then no one would know where it was hidden," she murmured. "And, of course, I'd be the first to forget."

So she rejected the proposal and never invited the taxidermist back. Whenever the plaster stuffing began to crumble from the moose's nose, she patched it up with adhesive tape. When Scotch Tape eventually appeared on the market, she switched to that. It made the moose look less wounded, she explained.

What finally killed Muzzy's ambitions as an interior decorator were Daddy's Russian prints. On one of his trips to St. Petersburg to sell the Czar a ship to replace another the Japanese had just sunk, he discovered the prints, dozens of them, and brought them home together with recipes for Russian borsch for Lizzy, records of Russian gypsy songs for the girls and Cossack uniforms for the boys.

The prints were huge affairs—about three by four feet—painted in vivid reds and purples. They depicted various episodes from Russian history beginning with the Varangian invasions, through the Tartar, Turkish and Polish invasions and ending with Napoleon's sack of Moscow, which showed soldiers in French uniforms throwing objets d'art out of palace windows and getting very drunk on looted wines.

From a hasty glance you might have gone away with the impression that all the Russians ever did was get invaded but a more thorough study showed that they also tortured serfs, lashed Volga boatmen, impressed peasants into the army and worshiped the Czar and the Patriarch of all the Russians, who dressed in very expensive ermine and cloth of gold.

Muzzy dutifully admired the gory prints, whereupon Daddy took them to town and a few days later brought them back mounted in heavy black frames. He announced he was going to hang them around and about the house.

He started hanging in the schoolroom. Then he lined the walls of the hall. He went up the front stairs, hanging as he climbed, and covered the second-floor corridors with the prints. He started up the third-floor stairs and by that time he was hanging them double, one above the other. When he had finally covered the walls of the third-floor halls, he found he still had half a dozen pictures unhung. So he stacked them in the attic and from time to time replaced the ones on the walls with those in the attic like a museum director revising his exhibits.

When he was through, it was impossible to raise your eyes at Kyneton without seeing a Russian being invaded, maimed, burned or beaten, except for the Czar and the Patriarch, who were being worshiped in their expensive ermine. Muzzy's dreams of a French château with delicious little oils of pastoral scenery were dashed for good. But the effect on us children was just as profound, particularly on the two youngest, Avis and me. We eventually ended up spending years in Moscow at the American Embassy.

When Hitler began his invasion of Russia in 1941 and the S.S. started stringing up and shooting down innocent Russian peasants, some of our friends in Moscow were mystified by the equanimity with which we looked at the news pictures and propaganda posters of German atrocities. The fact was it all seemed to us just a little *déjà vu.*

Somehow Muzzy managed to defend the drawing room from the Russian prints. Instead she furnished it with delicate tapestried chairs, spindly tables and fragile porcelain lamps. Little of this, however, retained its original form during our childhood. The tapestried upholstery was shredded by pets' claws, faded by the years and recolored by jam. The tables were propped in corners or against other bits of furniture so that their loose legs, broken leaves or missing drawers would not show. The lamps were glued, taped or simply tied together when they cracked and stood at odd angles with legs missing, waiting for someone to give them a slight nudge or stumble over their electric cords, which were carefully camouflaged on the floor like trip wires in a mine field.

One set of chairs held out much better than the rest largely because we never used them ourselves. They were known as "the booby traps" because their upholstered seats were held in place by a device so delicate that the slightest movement by the occupant sent him crashing through the bottom, his knees jackknifed against his chin, his hot tea pouring painfully down his shirt front.

The only time we used the chairs was when callers came against whom we had a grudge. Quietly so that Muzzy would not notice we would pull out one of the booby traps and offer it to our victim. Then we would retire into a corner and wait giggling for the inevitable crash. Usually one experience with a booby trap was enough to keep the victim away from Kyneton for a year or more.

While Kyneton was being put together, Muzzy and Daddy started producing the family in a nearby rented house. Although Muzzy was a member in good standing of the Ladies' Committee of the Bryn Mawr Hospital, it never occurred to her to go there except to visit frailer members of the human race.

As I was second to the last child, I remember the arrival only of Avis, the youngest. Probably my recollection is so vivid because I brooded about her arrival long afterward, as I was not at all convinced that Avis was really necessary.

We should perhaps have been tipped off by the visit of an old friend of Muzzy's who nursed us whenever we were sick. But all we were told was that Muzzy was having one of her headaches, and to keep the house quiet we were sent away to cook fudge in the bungalow at the foot of the property with the tenant, Mrs. Anderson. While we waited for the fudge to harden—it always took too long and sometimes never hardened at all—we caught sight of Dr. Gamble, the family doctor, driving up to the big house in his Model T. In the back seat, a small unfamiliar object was sitting alone.

Eager to welcome the visitor, we raced up to the house through the orchard and arrived just in time to see Dr. Gamble stop and get out. He opened the back door of the car where an infant was sitting erect and prim dressed in baby's clothes, a huge floppy white lace bonnet tied under her chin. He took her in his arms and disappeared into the house. A few minutes later we were told that Avis had officially arrived.

Avis still protests that my memories of her birth are imaginary. But then she too has been a bit fuzzy under similar circumstances. Once she herself was having a child at Bryn Mawr Hospital, Muzzy having reluctantly condoned her children's frailty. As her husband was on duty in Moscow, I went along and, after she had returned from the delivery room, visited her in her room.

She gazed at me groggily, waved her hand and murmured, "I want you to be best man."

With Avis, Muzzy finally called a halt. By then there were six of us at two-year intervals: Sissy born in 1903, then George, Buckety (a corruption of Buttercup—the name Sissy, the family poetess, gave her), then Betsy, myself and Avis.

In those days six were well above the quota for Episcopalians who by then had stumbled on the secrets of birth control. When an old friend remonstrated with Muzzy because of the size of her brood, his wife cut him down acidly:

"You collect polo ponies," she pointed out. "So why shouldn't Gertrude collect children?" We children found it a rather odd analogy but Muzzy did not mind. She loved horses.

When Sissy reached school age, Muzzy must have had misgivings about her own education for she took prompt steps to see that we had an adequate schooling. Getting together with her neighbors, especially Cousin Bessie Packard, who was raising four children herself across the road from Kyneton, she built a school on the property. She hired a schoolmistress and together with Cousin Bessie hand-picked the first class of seven students. By the time the last of us had graduated from Kyneton School, more than a hundred children were squeezed into the bungalow's little rooms.

The headmistress, Miss Laing, was a tiny but formidable lady with a great shock of gray hair piled on top of her head. But even the topmost strand was scarcely four feet off the floor. She came from the Scottish Highlands and spoke with a distinct burr. At singing class we sang only Scotch songs and our history lessons revolved chiefly about Bonnie Prince Charlie, Robert Bruce and other Highland heroes. But in other respects, our curriculum was more than adequate.

Naturally we had lots of athletics. Muzzy saw to that. We developed a fierce loyalty to Kyneton and created an imaginary rivalry with every other school in Philadelphia, blithely ignoring the fact that we never competed with any of them in sports or even in spelling bees.

My oldest sister, Sissy, wrote the school song, which we sang with conviction as though it were a hymn or the national anthem. It went to the tune of "The Bonnets of Bonnie Dundee" and it began:

Our school colors represent sunshine and hope
And whenever in ignorance blindly we grope,
We are lighted by sunshine and cheered by the hope
So hurrah for Kyneton School.

We even had a school cheer used irrespectively by all sides in any contest. It went:

Razzle-dazzle
Hazzle-dazzle
Sis-boom-bah!
Kyneton, Kyneton,
Rah-rah-rah.

On Commencement Day each spring we cheered each other till we were hoarse and sang the Kyneton School song till the tears ran down our cheeks. Miss Laing organized Commencement with such infinite pains that every pupil got at least one prize. Sometimes she had to stretch things rather far, like Third Best Effort in Singing. But she never left anyone out.

We always had a play at Commencement too. I was usually one of the rats in the "Pied Piper." A classmate once played the role of a table and got so worked up about it that he vomited all over himself.

Kyneton was nevertheless a much-sought-after school and applications always far exceeded the available desks even when it had grown to a hundred pupils, at which point the local fire marshal stepped in and called a halt. The admissions committee consisted of Muzzy and Cousin Bessie. Though they lived directly across the road from each other, they used the telephone for hours on end to weigh the qualifications of applicants—and of their parents. Some parents, not always good-naturedly, complained that it was easier to get into Harvard than into Kyneton.

Aside from children and servants Muzzy and Daddy stocked Kyneton with horses, donkeys, cows, pigs, and innumerable chickens, to say nothing of dogs and other pets.

When I was small, we had two dogs, Tinkle and Dickie. Dickie was supposed to be a setter. Tinkle never pretended to be anything. Later we had a Boston bull terrier called Iota, a disgusting little bitch but loved by Muzzy.

Then after I spent a year in England, I came home with a pair of Border terriers, a little-known breed distinguished by its skunk-like smell, fierce temper and "sporting instinct," which meant, in English jargon, a love of killing things. The bitch was already "having," as Muzzy called the state of pregnancy. The customs inspectors said they had never heard of the breed, which was not even listed by the Westminster Kennel Club. So they charged me two dollars and fifty cents apiece for importing mongrels. I was incensed and wrote the Westminster Club telling them what I thought of them. The club wrote back apologetically saying they would not only recognize the breed but would have a class for them at the next show in New York.

I immediately got my five dollars refunded by customs and to return the club's compliment entered the dogs in the show. By now the puppies had arrived so I entered them too.

But by the time the show took place, I was already enrolled as a plebe at West Point so Muzzy had to arrange to ship the whole pack to New York and hire a handler to show them. When *Time* ran a story with a picture of me in cadet gray as the owner of the latest breed at the show and winner of every class—best Border terrier dog, best bitch, best puppy and best of breed—it failed to point out that mine were the only Border terriers entered. As plebes at West Point were not supposed to be dog fanciers on the side, life on the Hudson was made so miserable for me that I wished I was across the river in Sing Sing.

At one point Kyneton also housed several prairie dogs, which my brother had brought back from El Paso. They were kept in the unused fireplace in the schoolroom. George promptly lost interest in them and it was left to

Muzzy to take care of them. They bit fiendishly and acquired a distressing habit of gnawing their way out of their cage and hiding behind the bookcases whence Muzzy, thickly gloved, would pull them out by the tail. But once a prairie dog refused to come out, so the tail came off in Muzzy's hand. Soon afterward the prairie dogs passed away, to everyone's relief.

Then a friend of mine brought back a parrot from South America and gave it to me for Christmas. The parrot learned to talk quickly enough but he also learned to bite even more ferociously than the prairie dogs. When I soon afterward went off to boarding school, the parrot was turned over to Sarah, the parlor-maid, for safekeeping. For decades thereafter he kept the household in confusion, seemingly answering the telephone when it rang, calling for John to bring the Ford around to the door, whistling for the dogs and imperiously summoning the servants—all in a heavy Irish brogue.

Someone also gave me a Brazilian bulbul. "Bulbul" is the Persian name for nightingale but the Brazilian variety substituted a raucous scream for the original's melodious song. My bulbul was supposed to come when you called him. Occasionally he did but usually he did not, which resulted in frantic searches through the neighboring woods. I took the bulbul to boarding school with me and once when he escaped I was allowed to skip classes till I found him. But only once. After the first escape he sat in the woods and screamed till recess. I usually managed to lure him back by displaying a meal worm between my fingers. I raised the worms in my room in a box of damp moldy flour—to the acute discomfort of my neighbors.

One summer when we went abroad, I gave the bulbul to a pet shop in Philadelphia to take care of. As soon as we came home, I hurried in to retrieve my beloved bird. But all that was left of him was in a little paper parcel stored in the shop's icebox. I deeply mourned the bulbul but fortunately I had brought back from Paris a pair of zebra finches who soon commanded my complete devotion.

I took them to boarding school with me too. There they laid eggs regularly but as the eggs had only a thin film of a shell they invariably broke when the lady finch set on them. From a book on how to raise zebra finches I learned they needed lime in their diets so I knocked a bit of plaster off the wall in my room, ground it up and put it in the birds' cage. Within a few days three eggs complete with hard shells appeared in their nest.

I calculated that they would hatch a day or two before the Christmas holidays. So I wrote Muzzy explaining the exciting development and announcing I would not be able to get home for the vacation as the baby zebra finches would be too young to travel.

As soon as she had read my letter, Muzzy put in a call to Dr. Drury, the rector of St. Paul's. Dr. Drury ordinarily frightened parents out of their wits but Muzzy regarded him with disdain if not contempt. Prior to his rectorship, the school had been run by two cousins, the Drs. Coit, and Muzzy had often spent weeks visiting them at the rectory. She therefore looked on their successor as something of an interloper. Besides, and this was perhaps her chief cause of disdain, Dr. Drury was Low Church.

When she got him on the telephone, she indicated that whereas she had nothing against the school's policy of encouraging the boys to raise pets, she thought it was going a bit far when a clutch of zebra-finch eggs threatened to disrupt all her plans for the family Christmas.

Dr. Drury readily agreed and I was duly summoned to his office. Not nearly so brave as Muzzy, I went in trembling. To my bewilderment Dr. Drury started with a little discourse on Saint Francis of Assisi and his birds, but then by easy stages he switched into a homily on filial love and duty. When he thought he had me sufficiently softened up, he delicately suggested that I could make a traveling cage to take the birds and their young back on the special Pullman train that in those days transported the boys home for holidays.

But I was unconvinced and pointed out that changes in temperature, atmosphere and feeding hours, which the journey would necessitate, would probably affect their health permanently if not fatally. Besides, I pointed out, my last grades in Manual Arts showed I was not much good at building things. The cage would probably fall apart on the way and Dr. Drury could easily imagine the calamitous confusion if the parent birds should get loose in the overcharged atmosphere of a Pullman car filled with boys going on vacation.

Dr. Drury, however, was not likely to capitulate to

one of "his boys," especially after the talk he had had with Muzzy. So he picked up the telephone and called for Mr. Trask, the carpentry teacher, and instructed him to drop whatever he was doing and cooperate with me in building a traveling cage. Then with a curt "Good morning" I was dismissed.

The cage I designed and Mr. Trask built was a masterpiece worthy of Rube Goldberg. It had glass panels to let in light but keep out drafts, wooden panels to keep out light when it was the bird's normal bedtime and stout wire-mesh panels to keep the finches in and mischievous boys' fingers out. It was a tremendous success except that of course someone opened all the panels at once on the Pullman, and for an hour or so there was pandemonium as the father zebra finch flew frantically from one end of the car to the other. Luckily he was caught without damage and replaced in the cage.

But alas even Dr. Drury could not foresee all the dangers of the Christmas holiday and certainly not the disaster produced by the oil furnace.

That autumn as the first cold northers began to blow, a friend had told Muzzy about a new invention—oil heating. Having frozen for twenty-five years in drafty Kyneton, she was more than eager to get this latest miracle of science.

Unfortunately the oil furnace had not yet been fully perfected and had one or two little bugs still not ironed out. Besides, John Nagle, who was put in charge of the furnace, had not yet fully grasped the mechanics of the Ford and was not ready for the next great step forward represented by the thermostat, the electric motor and the fuel pump, which Muzzy now had installed in the cellar.

Furthermore, I doubt if the oil furnace had ever been designed to cope with such problems as Kyneton's. All day and all night it would go on and off with a loud click and a flash that would dim the lights. And when it was in full stride, it let out a low ominous moan like an angry wild animal roaming about in the bowels of the house. But it did keep the house less cold if not warm and Muzzy was delighted.

During the holiday a beau of one of my sisters, resorting to the ancient strategy of befriending the younger brother, invited me to drive down with him to Atlantic City, where he was going on business. Atlantic City in late December was not a very gay place. Giant waves splashed over the deserted boardwalk while a bitter sea wind lashed spray in our faces and froze our bones. But still it was an adventure and I enjoyed it thoroughly, even forgetting to worry about the zebra finches, which I had left for the day in the spare room.

When we returned that evening, Kyneton from the outside seemed quite normal. But as we opened the front door, it was obvious that something ghastly had happened. The walls, the ceilings, the furniture and the curtains were black with soot and the air smelt horribly of oil fumes. Muzzy, looking as though she had a headache, was conducting Herbie Church, a cousin who handled our insurance, from room to room.

We interrupted to ask what had happened. Muzzy muttered, "The furnace."

"What did it do?" I asked.

"It exploded." she said dolefully. Then I remembered the zebra finches and dashed to the third floor. There on the bottom of the cage lay the two adult zebra finches and beside them their three young. My sister Betsy, thinking to console me, went to the piano and played "Bye Bye Blackbird," but I simply wailed louder. When I eventually recovered from my tears, I buried the babies in the garden but I sent the parents to the taxidermist. As I write this now, forty years later, the father zebra finch is watching me from his perch on the mantelpiece while the mother finch is gazing adoringly from a lower branch up at her spouse.

When all of us children had finally married and moved elsewhere, Kyneton continued to be a headquarters for Muzzy's grandchildren. Usually they loved to stay there for despite its plebeian atmosphere compared to Pembroke, it was still far more luxurious than their own homes. But it did have its drawbacks.

The strange noises under the roof, for example. They were so loud and eerie that the grandchildren living on the third floor were frightened to go to bed at night. They complained to Muzzy but she impatiently refused to believe the stories of sounds in the attic and told them to show pluck. Then her younger sister came to stay and she too complained of noises. Muzzy told her sister that she was too old to believe in ghosts. She was seventy.

But finally the noises got so loud that one night Muzzy herself, sleeping two floors below, heard them.

Next morning she sent for John and told him to climb up through the trap door and see what was going on under the roof. John hated heights, especially climbing up ladders, and he was terrified of deserted places like attics. But he was still more terrified of Muzzy so, trembling like a leaf under Muzzy's stern eye, he clambered up to the trap door, cautiously lifted it a few inches and peered into the gloomy loft. There was a moment's pause, then a stifled cry and John came tumbling down and lay crumpled up on the floor, pale and speechless.

Muzzy stared at him, bewildered. "Merciful patience, John," she said. "Whatever is the matter with you?"

John finally found his tongue, "There's six of 'em, Madam," he mumbled.

"Six of what?" Muzzy asked.

"Raccoons, Madam."

The raccoons were among the last of Kyneton's house pets.

SIX

Teatime

AUGUSTUS CAPPS was not the first servant at Kyneton but he was the oldest by far. He was born a slave in the South and during the Civil War had escaped to Philadelphia, where he settled and got a job as footman with Granny Wheeler, rising slowly to the eminence of butler. But then his rheumatism got so bad that he was unable to manage the big Pembroke household and was put out to pasture at Kyneton.

Once every two or three weeks he went to town to visit his children and grandchildren and his closest friend, John White, the headwaiter at Broad Street Station restaurant. The Whites and the Cappses in those days were among the most respected leaders of Negro society in Philadelphia. Whenever we were taken to lunch by Uncle Walter at Broad Street Station, White greeted us like minor royalty.

Originally Augustus lived in a room in the attic on the third floor, but as his rheumatism got worse and he was unable to cope with the two flights of stairs, Muzzy converted one of the jam closets in the cellar for him. Since he also tended the coal furnaces in the cellar, he found the arrangement quite satisfactory. Besides as he grew older, the drafts of Kyneton drove him to the cellar in winter in his spare time. There on a rocking chair beside the furnace he kept himself warm as he mused about the old days when Muzzy and then her children were small.

In summer he brought his rocking chair to the back porch where he sat by the hour smoking a battered old pipe. As children we often sat on the porch steps while he told stories about his Civil War experiences as a drummer boy. It was never clear which army, North or South, he served in but I'm inclined to think he served in both. When the stories ran out, he armed the four youngest of us with broomsticks and taught us the manual of arms or marched us around the back yard like a squad of soldiers.

He had a round smiling face and as the years passed his frequent grins became more and more toothless. From my earliest recollection he was always bald with only a little halo of curly gray hair around his pate. He was small and very bowlegged and as he grew older his legs bowed more and his height shrank.

One of Gus's duties was to deliver messages from Muzzy to John. In summertime he simply stood on the back steps and hollered over to the stable. But in winter when the stable doors were shut against the cold, he had to tramp through the snow to John's rocking chair by the stable stove.

Whether it was the sight of old Gus stumbling through the drifts leaning heavily on his stick or the hollering that bothered Muzzy, she finally felt obliged to have a telephone rigged up between the back hall and the stable. The electrician who installed it must have been a big man and he fastened it to the wall at a height convenient to himself. Unfortunately it was a good two feet above Augustus's head. It would have been simple enough to lower the phone but instead Muzzy sent for the carpenter and had a stepladder built up to it. Thirty years after Augustus died, the stepladder still stood by the wall under the worn-out telephone—a monument, or at least a pedestal, to our beloved Gus.

Another of Augustus's duties was to summon us to meals by sounding the gong. When he had the word from Lizzy, the cook, he appeared at the dining-room door, and then like a conductor before his orchestra, he reached for the baton, straightened his shoulders, pulled down his coat, raised his chin and deliberately, carefully struck the pipes, running up and down the scales twice. As the booming died away in the far corners of the house, silence again fell. Whatever we were doing we continued to do without interruption until Muzzy's voice called out that lunch was ready. Then from all over the house came whining protests: "But it's only the first gong."

Two minutes later, spurred by an impatient Lizzy,

Augustus reappeared and repeated the performance. At last, reluctantly, we put down our games and books and straggled into the dining room while Muzzy waited patiently to say grace until the last of us was in place behind our chairs, heads bowed, trying to switch our thoughts from whatever we had been up to to more spiritual matters. Muzzy, too, tried but sometimes like us she was unable to drive household chores from her mind.

One midday all of us had assembled around the table, heads bowed waiting for the grace, when the telephone rang and Augustus announced that Muzzy was wanted by Cousin Bessie Packard. We all groaned and Muzzy resignedly went to the phone in the hall, and for ten minutes she and Cousin Bessie discussed the problems of Kyneton School, the relative merits of horse or cow manure for the rose garden and as usual the latest family pregnancy.

Like the other inventions of the Machine Age we were then entering, Muzzy took to the telephone, or electric communicator as it was first called, with enthusiasm, exploiting it heartlessly. Like the car and unlike the horse, she knew it was tireless. And when it was out of order or the operator left her switchboard in Bryn Mawr or someone left the receiver off the hook upstairs, she was furious and would explode with "Thundering guns!"

However, unlike the Model T, our phone was one of the first in the neighborhood—the forty-sixth judging by the number Bryn Mawr 460. (The zero, Daddy said, was added by the telephone company just to show off.)

After the phone was installed, Muzzy began each day by checking in with her sisters, cousins, neighbors and eventually her married children with a quick rundown of the day's agenda, usually ending by arranging a rendezvous for later in the day when she could really go into things and tie up the loose ends of her thoughts.

We children, on the other hand, regarded the telephone as an infernal contraption to distract Muzzy's attention from our own more pressing problems—like eating, for example.

So we waited fidgeting and quarreling behind our chairs until Muzzy and Cousin Bessie were through. At last Muzzy hurried back to her place at the head of the table, bowed her head and said devoutly, "Bryn Mawr 460."

It was the last day of grace at Kyneton.

There was only one meal to which we were never summoned and were always on time: tea. After Granny died, the tea ritual moved from Pembroke to Kyneton. It began very ceremoniously and had a definite resemblance to the opening of High Mass at the Church of the Good Shepherd. Promptly at four-thirty Augustus appeared carrying a tablecloth. From a corner of the drawing room he brought out the tea table, its gate-legs and leaves flapping, and put it in front of Muzzy's chair. He spread the tablecloth and drew up a second table for the food. Then he hobbled out and a minute later reappeared carrying a silver platter on which the teakettle, cradled above a lighted lamp, teetered precariously as he made his way across the room. Behind him the parlormaid followed carrying a tray of teacups and food.

When Muzzy was trying very hard to live within her income, the food usually consisted of Ginger S's—jawbreaking cookies that we all loved though they occasionally chipped a tooth or pried a filling loose. But when she finally gave up all pretense of making do with what the bank doled out, the tea menu took a turn for the better. There were sandwiches and cookies, cinnamon buns and hot buttered scones and jam that always fell in sticky gobs on the Persian carpet, where it stayed until Iota, the unattractive Boston bull terrier, was summoned to lick it up. Iota did a good job, leaving only a small stain, but the stains were cumulative and over the decades the carpet, originally beige, took on a raspberry tinge.

Besides the children there were always one or two callers, and on Sundays the drawing room at teatime was often so crowded that the younger children were relegated to the schoolroom next door. Very seldom was anyone invited to tea. They just came. There were uncles and aunts, old friends and neighbors and cousins from all over the globe.

Often there were several cousins living in the house, whose families had moved out West or down South or to Canada and who were on holidays or in nearby schools or colleges or just visiting.

And then of course there were our friends whose parents had given up the tea habit or had never adopted it. Once a young man from New York appeared and after stuffing himself with tea and cake told Muzzy how much he enjoyed the novelty of serving tea in the middle of the afternoon. "Sometimes I have coffee between meals," he told her, "but I never before thought of tea." Muzzy looked at him agape as though he had just emerged from the jungle or the steppe. "How very interesting" was all she could think of to say.

For Muzzy, tea had been a part of her daily life since she was a child, and as long as she lived when four-thirty came around she had her cup whether she was motoring across the continent or flying across the ocean. Coffee was for breakfast and after dinner but tea and tea only was for teatime.

One afternoon my sister Betsy, who had recently married and was living in the ex-schoolhouse, called Muzzy frantically to the phone. She had been expecting her first child and now the birth pains were coming with alarming frequency. Could Muzzy possibly drive her to the hospital? Muzzy glanced at her watch. It was four o'clock, so she said, "Why, of course I will, my dear. I'll just tell Augustus to have tea a little early."

The child arrived minutes after Muzzy, her tea finished, got Betsy to the hospital.

Once the ceremony of bringing in the tea things was over and the servants had withdrawn, the atmosphere relaxed. While Muzzy poured, the children distributed the cups and then the food to the callers as they arrived. Sometimes Muzzy warned us in advance of visitors who had phoned to anounce their coming.

"Mr. Harrison is dropping by," she would say. "You know, the one who stutters. He's a very dear old friend of mine so please don't laugh when he talks. It's very rude."

It was a hopeless plea. As Mr. Harrison, very old indeed, hobbled into the room, he had hardly finished saying, "Gug-gug-gug-Gertrude, dud-dud-dud-dud-dear," when one by one we doubled up with giggles and hurriedly left the room, leaving Muzzy biting her lip to control her own laughter.

When Mr. Harrison had gone, we would get a lecture from Muzzy about the wickedness of laughing at others' infirmities. But the lecture was never too sincere because Muzzy herself had never learned to control her giggling spells—even in church.

The pew ahead of ours at the Church of the Good Shepherd was occupied by the Geyelin family. Old Mr. Geyelin was as bald as a shiny apple. Standing behind him, George one Sunday suddenly became entranced by the back of Mr. Geyelin's head and whispered something to Buckety. Buckety's shoulders began to shake with laughter. Trying to look severe, Muzzy scowled. "What is George doing?" she whispered. "He says Mr. Geyelin's head looks like strawberry ice cream," we told her. Muzzy looked at the bald pate and slowly the scowl disappeared. The corners of her mouth began to twitch, her shoulders heaved. She looked fixedly at the altar and tried to think of something sad. But it was useless and in a moment the whole pew rocked with silent giggles while the rest of the congregation stared disapprovingly.

What could have got into the Thayers?

Muzzy also had a hopeless weakness for mixing up names.

"Remember," she would warn us, "Mrs. Sidebottom is coming to tea—I only hope I can remember it myself." But when Mrs. Sidebottom walked in, Muzzy as likely as not would introduce her as Mrs. Topbottom and reduce us all to helpless giggles. Then she too would try to hide her face in her napkin but her shaking shoulders gave her away. Finally to restore order she would point to the dog. "Charlie, put Iota out. She's about to make a mess in the corner." She could not even get her own children's names straight and when she wanted one of us she would call out the entire roster: "George, Charlie, Buckety, Avis, Sissy—I mean Betsy, you're wanted to the phone."

And when some poor shy creature fell through the bottom of one of the booby-trap chairs, with his chin between his knees and a cupful of tea in his lap, she would do her best to look distressed and sympathetic but she usually ended up rocking with laughter followed by a deep fit of remorse for her bad manners.

Though the teatime callers were not always scintillating or even interesting, Muzzy welcomed them all—all except one. She was the grandmother of a young man in the Diplomatic Service and therefore considered she had a bond in common with Muzzy, two of whose children were in the Service. Mrs. X was a garrulous old hen, so boring that even Muzzy could not stomach her, and when Muzzy saw her car driving up, she would send word to the front door that she was out and then, lest she be telling a lie, dart out a French window onto the back terrace until she heard Mrs. X's car depart.

When Mrs. X telephoned, Muzzy had a similar stratagem. "Tell her I'm lying down," she would call to whoever answered the phone and to make good her word she sprawled out full length on the floor till the message was delivered. I suspect that Mrs. X came to think of Muzzy as a bloody liar but that didn't bother Muzzy. It was her conscience, not Mrs. X, that she was concerned about.

Except for Mrs. X, Muzzy was no snob. Sometimes when an unfamiliar name came up in conversation, she might ask a bit vaguely, "Do we know them?" But I never heard her ask, "Does one know them?"

As the years went by, the older callers grew fewer and fewer but their places were taken by friends of ours. Long after we had all left Kyneton, they would come and perch on the fire seat beside Muzzy and tell her their troubles. The fire seat was made of cast iron and covered with a thin hard cushion from which horsehair sprouted through numerous rips in the leather cover. It was low and very narrow, so that you had to perch on it with your bottom hanging only inches from the flames behind. It could not possibly have been less comfortable but it was the only place where you could carry on a private discussion with Muzzy, who was otherwise surrounded by tea tables.

The reasons for our friends coming and roasting their backsides by the fire were as varied as the friends were themselves. There was Howard, for example, older than most of us but much younger than Muzzy—a bachelor, shy but articulate. He came out of sheer loneliness. Often he stayed after the others had gone and the tea things had been cleared away. Then he would read aloud to Muzzy by the hour, content to have an attentive listener and reluctant to go home to his big rambling empty house where there was nothing to do but get potted.

There was Bobby, once a beau of Betsy's, a New Yorker, a little slow but charming. He had first sat on the fire seat and told Muzzy about his problems of getting into college, and then the problem of staying in and eventually graduating. Later there were the problems of a marriage gone wrong. To all his woes Muzzy listened, clucking sympathetically, never scolding but occasionally asking pointed questions like "Do you think that decision was quite right?" Muzzy was convinced that if you just tried hard enough you could do anything. So she always encouraged them. "I know you can make it if you just try" was a favorite expression.

I can never remember Muzzy talking about herself. She never lectured, never suggested that she knew the answers or that her age had given her superior wisdom. But to her children and some of the cousins whom she treated as such she could be a cutting critic. Her comments to us were often poison barbs, though shot with a gentle, almost apologetic gesture.

"I did not like your last book as much as the one

before," she once told me when I came home after a long absence. I asked her why.

"It seems to me you're beginning to take yourself a little seriously," she answered. She never took herself seriously.

There was David, who had come with a letter of introduction from England to learn the conservative practices of Philadelphia bankers. He had a bad complexion, worse teeth and a defensive air of superiority. But Muzzy liked him because he was English, and did her best to explain the customs and foibles of America to him.

Hunky was quite a different type. A football-playing friend of George's, from the Pennsylvania coal-mine area, he was without complexes or worries and as open as his face was wide and flat. He came to have a good time and while his very large behind was toasting in the fire he regaled Muzzy with endless funny stories. His repertoire was occasionally a bit repetitive, but since Muzzy always forgot a joke the moment she had heard it, she laughed just as hard the second and third time it was told.

Sam had a drinking problem. Muzzy disapproved strongly of drinking too much but she considered habitual drunks as victims of an unfortunate ailment and to be pitied, not scolded. So she listened sympathetically to Sam's confessions, suggesting remedies and encouraging him to show courage in the face of his weakness. Once when Sam moved over beside me to make room for someone else at the fire seat, he whispered, "I don't know why I tell your mother things I seldom even admit to myself." The reason was, of course, that he could trust Muzzy's discretion. We had long since been taught not to eavesdrop on those whispered conversations on the fire seat and Muzzy herself never mentioned them except, probably, in silence at church or at her bedside prie-dieu. When she went to early church—which was three of four times a week—she always took along with her prayer book a little black notebook in which she listed anniversaries to be remembered in her prayers and cryptic reminders to pray for divine intercession on behalf of her troubled friends.

Lorrimer was an extremely bright scientist but there his talents ended abruptly. Like others, he had originally come courting one of the girls, but when his suit was unmistakably rejected, he came to talk to Muzzy. His conversation was confined to detailed dissertations on the latest electronic devices he had invented. Muzzy as usual listened attentively and since she never asked for explanations Lorrimer was convinced she understood him completely and had a natural genius for electronics. Actually she never learned the difference between a volt and a liter. When he finally stopped talking and left, to the relief of the rest of us, Muzzy would sigh sorrowfully and murmur to herself, "He's so nice and so bright—if I only knew what he was talking about I'm sure he'd be fascinating."

And finally there was Andy, a hardy-perennial caller.

I can't remember how he joined the company, but he was probably brought to tea by some other friend and thereafter he regularly accepted the invitation to come again. No one knew anything about his background except that he had studied to be an architect but had failed and ended up a draftsman in an engineering office. His mother was in an old-people's home and practically his entire salary was spent in supporting her there. He himself lived in a bleak Philadelphia rooming house, and so far as we knew his only outings were to Kyneton. He always took the Paoli Local to Villa Nova Station and walked the remaining mile to our place. I can still remember him puffing up the drive, his round face red and sweaty and grinning. In his hand he clutched a bouquet of wilting wild flowers he had picked along the roadside on the way from the station. Andy came to be cheered but he was so desperately determined to be gay and disguise the drabness that his dreary life had imprinted on him that his efforts to amuse us were as pathetic as an unfunny clown's. Muzzy was not only sorry for him but genuinely fond of him and did her very best to cheer him, laughing loudly if not always sincerely at his dreary O. Henry-like tales of life in his rooming house, which he always concluded with a raucous blast of laughter.

Andy turned up about once a month and we often wondered what he did on those other weekends. He sometimes came at Christmas and he invariably showed up on Easter Sunday, trudging slowly up the drive clutching his wilted bouquet, which he thrust at Muzzy with a forced laugh meant to indicate that he couldn't afford to buy her something better.

On Christmas Eve activities in the drawing room at Kyneton reached a mad crescendo. The script, lyrics, music and direction were exclusively Muzzy's—a medley of Early American, Old English, tribal German and other pagan and Christian customs. Muzzy combined them into a rich extravaganza heartily deplored by her bank.

As long as Daddy was alive, he turned Christmas over to Muzzy and enjoyed himself exclusively as a spectator. Like every father, he had as much fun playing with our toys as we did. The goat cart was an exception. The wheels were held on by bolts that went counterclockwise and before he discovered it he had skinned both his thumbs and almost exhausted his vocabulary of swear words.

Preparations for Christmas began many weeks—but never enough weeks—before the holiday. The first step was drawing up the list of probable guests. The last year's list was a starter and the idea was always to pare it down. This year Aunt Bessie had moved to England. Cousin Henry was off in Africa and Marjorie and her brood were in Hawaii. That meant six less—a mere thirty-eight in all. But then young Syd was back from a year in Europe and there was the annual crop of young ones who had reached party age. Muzzy considered anyone over three as old enough. That brought it up again to forty-four. And of course the additions by marriage—another three. Would Andy turn up? Better be prepared. In the end the list usually came to about fifty plus extras. The extras were those Muzzy might have forgotten, from whom presents with blank name tags were set aside.

Then came the selection of suitable presents. This year again the accent was on frugality. Mr. van Meter at the bank had stressed the point. One pair of evening gloves each for the aunts and a tie for the uncles. Except, of course, Cousin Hannah. She was so poor Muzzy always threw in a half-dozen pairs of silk stockings. And Uncle Walter, the favorite uncle, always got fur-lined gloves because he motored so much.

We children had been drawing up our individual requests for months. Mine included a goat and a goat cart. Muzzy put a firm line through the goat and suggested that Uncle Walter get me the cart. Similar deletions and assignments were made in the others' lists.

For the servants it was relatively easy. The women got smocks, the men shirts. John Nagle got shirts with detachable stiff collars and Augustus got half a dozen with stiff fronts and wing collars. Ever since Muzzy had first staffed Kyneton, it had been her dream to see the chauffeur-coachman in a clean stiff collar and the butler in a white stiff shirt. But it was a vain dream despite the Christmas presents. When Augustus died, we discovered a heap of unopened boxes tucked away in a corner of the jam cellar, each with half a dozen brand-new stiff shirts.

Then came the actual buying. Every day or so Muzzy

drove to town and trudged through Wanamaker's, Strawbridge & Clothier's, Jacob Reed's and occasionally Caldwell's, the jewelers, looking, selecting, ordering and, of course, charging. And a few days later the delivery vans would bring mountains of boxes that were stored in the spare room, where in great secrecy Muzzy unwrapped, rewrapped and tagged their contents.

We children too were feverishly active during this period for each of us had to make a present for Muzzy and Daddy—an embroidered doily, a hemstitched washrag, an initialed towel or even a clay birdbath baked in the school handicraft shop. We also had to get presents for each other. As a child I was very careful with my money and it is reported that one year I gave each of my sisters and my brother a five-cent Hershey bar and an *Evening Bulletin* of the week before. I always shopped early.

Finally there was the tree. Muzzy inevitably bought one that was too big and John Nagle, who installed it, invariably cut it down to size from the top so that it looked like a shapeless pillar holding up the drawing-room ceiling. It was my job to fix the lights, involving a last-minute rush to Bryn Mawr to get extra bulbs to replace the broken ones, for if one went out they all did. In deference to Muzzy's pyromaniac tendencies there were also real candles, which each year threatened to burn up the entire tree.

Then late on Christmas Eve morning there was a wild scramble to put on the decorations. Each of us fought and snatched and criticized and argued about the proper technique for draping the tinsel. (George liked to throw it at the tree. Sissy insisted it should be hung strand by strand.) Finally when we were finished, we were banned from the drawing room while Muzzy arranged the piles of presents for each of us.

On Christmas Eve, and only Christmas Eve, tea was served in the dining room. In addition to the sandwiches, cinnamon buns and scones there was ice cream and cake. At four o'clock, after a final checkup by the nurses on our party dresses and suits, we filed downstairs and began to welcome the guests. First came Uncle Charlie and his wife, Auntie. We greeted them effusively for Uncle Charlie always gave us each a five-dollar gold piece and every year we hoped he'd make it ten. Then came Uncle Syd and his wife, Aunt Elise, and Uncle Walter. Then Uncle Harry appeared, white-haired, very handsome and erect, dressed like a rich banker—which he was till the crash. We would rush toward him until we spotted two small creatures behind him and stopped dead in our tracks. It was the Sidebottom boys, children of Uncle Harry's sister-in-law. Each year they turned up. Each year we forgot them and each year it meant that one of us (usually myself) had to sacrifice a couple of presents to provide them with gifts, for Muzzy's extras were only for grownups. I hated the Sidebottoms. And I loathed the very name. They must have loathed it too because for a time they tried to improve it by pronouncing it "Seedy-Butom," with the accent on the last syllable, but that never took and they gave it up.

When the last guests had been served tea, we clustered

around Muzzy counting them up, identifying the extras and resentfully noting the absentees. We all believed that Christmas Eve at Kyneton was not only the greatest event on earth but that attendance was obligatory. Anyone so perverse as to stay away was not simply crazy but a traitor to boot. If Cousin Andrew did not show up, a state of cold war would exist between us till he made amends.

Now finally came the great moment. Muzzy slipped off to light the candles and then called in the guests, who assembled in front of the fire seated in extra chairs from the dining room. We children waited in the schoolroom next door. Then word was sent to "the back" that all was ready and the servants who had gathered there with their families diffidently tiptoed in and took their places in the back of the drawing room—standing, of course.

Last of all we children marched in and stood in front of the tree, casting surreptitious glances behind us at our particular pile of presents. I saw what was obviously a goat cart draped in Christmas paper. But where was the goat? Sissy gave the pitch and we burst into song—in German. While Muzzy beamed and our relatives looked puzzled, we went through "Stille Nacht." Then we sang "Adeste Fideles" in Latin and they nodded wisely to show they recognized the language. When we sang "Good King Wenceslaus," they brightened up a little but not very much as only Sissy could carry a tune.

There was a brief silence when the carols were over and then from upstairs came the sound of a bell. It was the bell used to summon us when we played outdoors, but this time we recognized it as Santa Claus's. Each year some unfortunate friend was dragooned for this role. He was dressed in a slightly ragged costume, white whiskers glued to his chin, a pillow stuffed under his belt and a large swig of whisky poured down his gullet by way of consolation. Some Santa Clauses managed to steal several large swigs. They were always the best.

Santa came in carrying a great sack of presents, which Muzzy had tried to arrange in order of protocol so that the seniors got their presents first, but it didn't always work and often the first present was for Johnny Nagle or Mary Elizabeth, the housemaid's daughter. Then Muzzy hurried forward, stuffed the present back into the sack and found one for Uncle Charlie.

While the presents were being distributed, we children waited anxiously peering behind us at our piles. Where was that goat? I wondered anxiously. When it finally came the servants' turn, Muzzy herself called out the names:

"Jimmy Mullen . . ."

"Annie Mullen . . ."

"Mrs. Mullen . . ." And then:

"Mullen," as the gardener, sweating profusely, came forward, his agonized face twisted with embarrassment. Most of the guests smiled in admiration at Muzzy's quaint demonstration of democracy in action. But others were less enthusiastic, regarding it as creeping socialism.

At last it was our turn and we dived under the tree to our piles, ripping away the paper from our presents. Somehow it never occurred to us that Santa Claus brought presents for the guests only—ours were already there. Once again I searched for the goat but when I discovered the army field telephone, which I had never dreamed I would get, the goat was temporarily forgotten.

An hour later it was all over. The servants had returned to "the back" and now the guests began to depart —reluctantly, we always thought. It never entered our minds that some of them might have looked on Kyneton Christmas Eve as the ordeal of the year. Nor could we imagine their grim thoughts as they stopped their cars on the way home to let their young throw up the excess ice cream and cake they had consumed.

Finally it was time to clean up. Seized with a momentary passion for economy, Muzzy made us carefully fold up all the usable Christmas paper. The rest she casually piled into the fireplace where it blazed up, usually setting the chimney afire. Once, as I've mentioned, the sparks set fire to the sleeping-porch roof and we had to send for the Bryn Mawr fire engines but to Muzzy's secret sorrow we never had a really good conflagration at Kyneton except for the pastures Muzzy herself set ablaze.

Now it was our turn for headaches and periodically one of us made a dash for the toilet under the stairs. Hot, sticky and exhausted, I thought again about the goat. I asked Muzzy why Santa had forgotten it. Muzzy too was having one of her "splitters" and she answered a little wearily that she thought I had enough pets with my pony, the parrot and the bulbul.

That night when I said my prayers, I secretly told the Virgin Mary I wished she had been my mother for I was sure she would have seen to it that I got the goat.

As we grew older and the Church of the Good Shepherd got higher and higher in its ritual, we took to going to Midnight Mass. It killed two birds with one stone, for it demonstrated our piety and relieved us of having to get up early for church on Christmas Day. For brother George, the latter was the decisive reason. Basically Low Church, he regarded the elaborate ceremonies as a little funny. One Christmas he solemnly took a walking stick to Midnight Mass. He was sitting at the end of the pew as the brilliant procession went by. First came the censer bearers, swinging their urns of incense on long chains. Then came the choir at full war strength, bellowing out the Christmas anthems, and finally in the rear, resplendent in glittering robes, came the rector, Father Townsend, attended by two magnificent acolytes.

Suddenly one of the censer bearers stopped and began to wrestle with the chain he was swinging. Behind him the procession came to a milling, shuffling halt. As the congregation peered around in consternation to find the cause of the delay, an acolyte came forward and untangled the chain, which somehow had wrapped itself around a walking stick. Muzzy was mortified but Father Townsend never discovered how the stick got into the act.

Still Christmas was not over. There was another Old English custom Muzzy had not yet exploited. Before we went to bed sick and tired on Christmas Eve, each of us hung our stocking on the mantel over the fireplace in the day nursery. Bright and early Christmas morning we woke up Muzzy and Daddy, and still in our pajamas we filed into the nursery to find the stockings bulging with more presents—the smaller ones that might have got lost under the tree, like cuff links and earrings and necklaces. For filler Muzzy used a liberal supply of tangerines, nuts, hard candy and, when everything else had run out, tissue paper.

This last ritual over, we dressed, breakfasted and got ready for church—provided we had not already done Midnight Mass. While Daddy was still alive, we often walked (or rather marched) to church in column of twos, with Daddy bringing up the rear shouting commands and counting out the pace. It made the two miles seem like a mere few hundred yards. Daddy went to church only on Christmas and Easter and then he rather shocked us by seeming to sleep during the sermon. But when we got home and were devouring the roast turkey, we would be amazed—and occasionally even more shocked—at Daddy's critique of what Father Townsend had preached. Muzzy did not always agree with his comments.

Often after church we visited the churchyard to decorate the graves. When flowers had been put on the graves of the Thayer and the Wheeler grandparents and great-grandparents and deceased uncles and cousins,

Muzzy made a final checkup to see that no one was forgotten.

Sometimes a little cry would burst from her lips. "There's dear little Susan," she would say, pointing to a tiny headstone. "She's so lonesome there off in the corner." Then she would take a few flowers from her father's grave and put them on little Susan's.

Actually little Susan was a sister of Muzzy's who had died at birth but she had become a legendary figure endowed with every virtue. Whenever Muzzy and her sisters got into arguments as children, little Susan's silent vote from the grave was always claimed by both sides. So now little Susan had her flowers and we all trooped home.

At last it was over—at least the ceremonial part of Christmas—and it was time to go outdoors and play touch football or ice hockey or, if the snow was deep enough, coast on the back hill till teatime.

SEVEN

Director of Athletics

DADDY, A FANATIC on sports, spent all his free time at home, teaching us the rudiments of catching footballs, throwing baseballs, riding and even shooting. He built a rifle range at the foot of the property that was the terror of our neighbors. He gave my brother George a high-powered rifle and as a consolation he gave me a .38-caliber horse pistol. It was so heavy I had to use both hands to aim it.

To develop our muscles he also built what was probably one of the first open-air jungle gyms. You couldn't buy them ready-made then so Daddy brought home some lengths of galvanized iron pipe from the shipyard and screwed them together to make a pair of parallel bars, a high bar, a swing for the smaller children and what seemed to us a terrifyingly high crossbar for the flying trapeze.

Muzzy objected to his putting them up on the front lawn so he erected them in the back yard off the kitchen where Lizzy raised her chickens.

The jungle gym was economical and sturdy and should have developed a great team of gymnasts. The only trouble was the iron pipes were far too large for our small hands and far too slippery to get a grip on. Besides, the rings on the trapeze were hung on what must have been anchor chains for they were so heavy you couldn't make them swing. Another drawback was that Lizzy's chickens used the bars as perches and covered them with chicken manure.

The trapeze rig eventually served a useful purpose whenever we slaughtered a pig. After the pig had been dispatched by a sharp blow between the eyes, he was strung up on the anchor chains by his hind feet while the butcher from Bryn Mawr slit his throat and built a fire under him to singe off his hair.

Years later when we had no more pigs, Muzzy tried to take down the equipment but it was so firmly embedded in concrete that she had to send for the plumber to cut it down. Daddy built things to last.

Our principal sport when we were small was riding. Daddy believed firmly that the only way to develop a good seat on a horse was to ride bareback. So none of us was allowed the comfort of a saddle till we reached our teens. Daddy was a stern drillmaster at the City Troop Armory, where he made the recruits bounce around in circles bareback for hours, and he was determined to be just as severe with his children. The results were mixed.

Some of us ended up competent horsemen. Others developed a psychotic loathing for riding and took up cross-country walking.

Daddy was not exclusively to blame for the aversion of some of his children to riding. The baby donkey had a lot to do with it. Daddy had acquired a jenny donkey for my brother George. She was relatively docile and George managed her satisfactorily. But then one spring John Nagle announced to Daddy that the donkey was pregnant. Daddy, incredulous, dismissed the idea as an Irish-Catholic myth. But despite her supposed virginity, the donkey eventually produced a foal. Daddy was furious and demanded to know what God-damned jackass was responsible. But John was silent. Daddy eventually calmed down and consoled himself by naming the baby donkey William Jennings Bryan.

The mystery of the apparently virgin birth was not cleared up till long after Daddy died. Among the neighbors whose fields joined ours were the Robertses. The Roberts boys as children formed a rival gang to ours and we were always at war. Only after we grew up and George, then married, bought the old Roberts house did we become good friends. Then and only then did Rad Roberts confess that he had briefly owned a jackass when we had the jenny. One Halloween night he slipped the jackass into the paddock where our jenny was grazing and the marriage was speedily consummated. When we confronted John Nagle with Rad Roberts' confession, John smiled sheepishly.

"Sure and I knew it all along," he said. "But it wasn't

for me to be telling your father." After all as custodian of the jenny's virginity he had his pride, to say nothing of his fear of Daddy's wrath.

Though William Jennings Bryan inherited none of his mother's docility, he was assigned to Buckety, then about ten years old. It was war from the beginning and a dirty war at that. Daddy ostensibly allied himself with Buckety but Buckety often wondered whether the alliance was helpful. Whenever the donkey misbehaved, Daddy applied a stout stick to his rump. Thereupon the donkey would buck, bolt or both and Buckety would end up with a hard thud on the ground.

Whenever they came to a ford, Daddy would warn, "Don't let him roll."

Buckety drove her heels into the donkey's sides, cracked him with her whip and pleaded hysterically as they entered the water. But inevitably as they got to the deepest part, the donkey slowed, stopped, bent his front knees, sank into the refreshing stream and with great deliberation rolled over, taking Buckety with him. Behind, Daddy swore as he ripped a branch from a tree. When he applied it to the donkey, the beast jumped up and tore off at a gallop leaving Buckety soaked and tearful, knee-deep in the rushing water. The routine seldom changed. Buckety was one of those who eventually became a cross-country walker.

After George went off to boarding school, both donkeys were given away and a Shetland pony was bought for me. Then Daddy and I went riding in the surrounding country every Sunday morning for three or four hours. When the weather was good, Muzzy and the other children and their friends often joined us on horses rented from a livery stable. Sometimes we were as many as nine or ten good, fair and indifferent riders. Daddy was still a stern master, and if one of the horses balked at crossing a stream or passing an automobile, he would take a stick to its rump until it relented and, dashing past the obstacle, galloped off across country, its passenger screaming bloody murder.

If the victim was one of her own children, Muzzy set her jaw and watched silently praying that her offspring would demonstrate the pluck if not the horsemanship she expected. But if it was some city friend who had never before been astride a horse, she would moan distressfully as the horse and rider disappeared over the hill. Sometimes, just to make matters worse I would race after the runaway to try to catch its rein in a Wild West imitation of my hero William S. Hart. Naturally the runaway simply ran faster and frequently it all ended with the passenger rolling in the dirt. Then another mad race ensued to catch the riderless horse. Daddy and I loved our Sunday rides but I'm not sure about all the others.

Occasionally Daddy took George and me camping and taught us how to choose a camp site, build a campfire and make a shelter out of rushes and pine boughs. He always had a pup tent. He even taught us how to cook. His specialty was a goulash of eggs, bacon and potatoes.

More often he took the entire family on an evening picnic in the unspoilt countryside. The prerequisites for a picnic ground were a view to the west so that we could watch the sunset and a high hill inaccessible by Model T so that the heavy wicker picnic hampers had to be hand-carried the last half mile or so. Generally the spot Daddy chose was infested with mosquitoes and caressed by a fickle wind.

While Muzzy and the girls spread the rugs and the tin picnic plates, I helped Daddy collect wood and start the fire. It was always an exciting operation as Daddy insisted on using no paper and only one match. The result was that he spent the first half hour or so on his stomach blowing into the glowing embers or stooping over the fire fanning it with his old tweed cap and all the time cursing in low but vigorous tones.

When finally we had eaten and settled down to watch the sunset, the wind would shift, blowing the smoke from the smoldering fire into our faces, or else the mosquitoes would swarm over us. Then Daddy would produce his citronella bottle and spread the oil over us in the vain but unshakable hope that it would repel the visitors. We always looked forward with wild enthusiasm to picnics with Daddy.

When Daddy died in 1923, he left Muzzy with six children aged from twenty-one to eleven. After twenty-three years of marriage, Muzzy found herself saddled with a host of problems that Daddy had always handled and that she had never even known existed. There were household accounts, wages, bank accounts, budgets and taxes to which she had scarcely given a thought in her life.

At first Uncle Charlie and then my brother George coached her in bookkeeping and the elements of budgeting. Her arithmetic improved a bit but her efforts to live on a budget were hopeless from the start. Every month she would appeal to Uncle Charlie or George, and after them to Mr. van Meter, the bank trustee, explaining that a number of bills had inexplicably turned up for which there were no funds. She was never personally extravagant, but when it came to running Kyneton, she operated as though it were a free and lavish youth hostel. And of course there were presents—not just at Christmas and birthdays but whenever anyone was hard up or Joe over in London needed funds to meet a bad check. And finally there was her wanderlust—racing around the world with half a dozen children and their friends in tow.

But far more important to her than the unexpected new responsibilities of management was the role she inherited from Daddy as director of athletics. She was well-equipped for the job. Not only was she a superb horsewoman but she was an excellent tennis player and a fiendishly good croquet player.

She and her sisters had learned field hockey in England and they brought back their sticks and equipment to Philadelphia where they helped get it started. In fact the Wheeler sisters were generally regarded as the field-hockey stars of the area.

When the wife of the founder of Drexel Institute, a girls' school, offered a cup for a field-hockey tournament, she invited the Wheeler sisters to make up a team to represent the institute, doubtless to lend tone to the event. None of them had ever been inside the institute's walls but they accepted enthusiastically and formed a team that included Muzzy and Aunt Nee, who was staying at Pembroke after her brief marriage to Uncle Max. The Wheeler girls won handily. Some of the other participants were puzzled by the Wheeler sisters' qualifications to play for the institute and one sportswriter specifically questioned the credentials of "the tall Countess" who had starred. It was probably the first time the Philadelphia sporting world had been confronted by ringers and they were more tolerant of them than they would have been a generation later. And anyway Mrs. Drexel was delighted.

Even after Muzzy was married, she kept on with her games. Every Monday night when Daddy went to the armory to drill with the City Troop, Muzzy went to the parish house where she coached the young women of the church in basketball, which was considered exclusively a girls' game in those days.

When Muzzy was young, Victorian fashions emphasized modesty but ignored mobility. Skirts were ankle low and shoes ankle high. Sleeves came well below the elbow and hats flopped over the eyes. An exception was made for field hockey, when the girls were allowed to wear middy blouses and flowing bloomers—over heavy woolen stockings, of course.

Another exception was for bathing, when skirts could rise almost to the knees, the legs modestly covered in black stockings, and bathing caps consisted of full black bonnets that came down over the ears. But you could not wear these risqué bathing costumes anywhere in public. On the Isle of Wight where Muzzy bathed in the sea, the ladies had to change into their bathing costumes in bathhouses on wheels drawn by horses, which took them out into the sea. Then the horses modestly withdrew and the ladies slipped unseen into the surf.

The purpose of this elaborate operation was obviously to spare any men who might be about from getting evil thoughts. To compensate for these restrictions, the gentlemen of the day often maintained private brothels affiliated with their exclusive gentlemen's clubs. But the more discreet Philadelphians went to New York once a week "to visit their barber." Muzzy knew nothing of these goings on until the more candid memoirs and novels about the Victorian and Edwardian ages were published in the twenties and the thirties. Then Muzzy caught on fast. By the time she was ninety, her eyes were wide open and when I accused her then of having been an admirer of Queen Victoria, who presided over these moral fashions, she said with an impatient snort, "That musty old prude!"

When Muzzy took over as director of athletics, Sunday riding was replaced by tennis. She wanted a professional to build a court at Kyneton but Uncle Charlie forbade such extravagance. So she decided to do it herself. She had the gardeners level a patch of the pasture near the house. Then she set the six of us children to work finishing the court.

It was grueling work, sifting the dirt to remove the stones and pebbles, then raking it smooth and then endlessly dragging a heavy cast-iron roller back and forth across it. Sometimes to pack the earth we sprinkled water on it but then it stuck to the roller, leaving gaping wounds on the surface. So Muzzy ordered cartloads of sand, which we sprinkled so liberally that the court looked like a bathing beach.

But eventually a fairly flat surface emerged and then we set to work digging postholes and stringing chicken wire for backstops. At first Muzzy was very frugal with the chicken wire, but when the toll of lost tennis balls mounted, she consented to enlarging the cages.

Finally she went to town and bought a box of tape lines at Spalding's. On the back of the box was a diagram showing how the court should look when it was properly laid out. For several days we struggled with the tapes, measuring, stretching and arguing endlessly. But each time we had the lines laid, they came out lopsided or they failed to meet or overlapped or the service line ran diagonally across the court. In the end we settled on a compromise between the model diagram and the tapes to make at least the semblance of a doubles court. There were few right angles and none of the corners met. The tapes were fastened into the ground with wire staples that frequently struck stones and refused to sink home, so we either hammered them over or let them stick up an inch or two. Later we found them useful when playing against strangers who did not know where the more dangerous ones were lurking to trip them up.

When everything was ready, Muzzy went back to town and came home with an armful of assorted rackets and six tennis balls. Within a day or two most of the balls had disappeared in the tall grass behind the backstops so thereafter she bought them by the dozen.

From then on, every morning Muzzy took us out into the sweltering sun in pairs and batted balls at us. When she had learned to play tennis as a child, it was considered unladylike to raise one's arm above the shoulder. So she always served underhand. But it was a vicious serve that began a few inches off the ground, shot like a bullet low over the net and scarcely bounced an inch as it flew past our rackets.

Muzzy never softened her service or slowed her return, no matter how young or inexperienced we were. She considered it unsporting if not downright dishonest to let her opponent win even when it was her favorite grandchild. The only encouragement we ever had was when on rare occasions she congratulated us for a good stroke.

When Sunday tennis took over from Sunday riding, Kyneton was busier than ever—provided of course it had not rained in the preceding day or so. For rain reduced the court to a muddy swamp and washed away the bank so that the sidelines were left hanging in space. All Sunday morning we children raked and scraped and rolled and hammered at protruding staples in the blazing sun.

As soon as lunch was over, friends and neighbors began to assemble either to play or to watch. Only the older and better of us children were actually allowed to participate. The rest of us chased the balls that flew over the chicken wire or that rolled under it into the field. Muzzy presided, playing occasionally but usually arranging sides after each set.

To keep us on our toes, one of the regular players, Jack Groome, the son of Captain Groome, who was captain of the City Troop in the Spanish-American War, and later himself a captain, offered an ingenious system of rewards. For every eight balls retrieved, each of us was entitled to an ice-cream soda. The ice-cream soda scores were cumulative and were paid off at one sitting in the autumn when Jack drove us down to Pricket's Drug Store in Rosemont in his Buick. While we sat at the fountain and gobbled up our sodas, Jack marched back and forth behind us checking to see that we consumed our full share. We seldom did. Muzzy never attended these nauseating feasts. She stayed at home and got a splitting headache just thinking about them.

The person who probably suffered most on tennis Sundays was Lizzy, the cook. As soon as she had cleaned up the lunch things, she had to get tea ready. That done she sat down, her hands folded in her lap, and waited tensely for orders for supper. How many would there be? Was there food enough in the larder?

In those days before cans and deep freezes we raised our own vegetables, slaughtered our own chickens and pigs, produced our own eggs and milk and butter and baked our own bread. Lizzy, the soul of economy, held the larder supplies to a minimum and kept our food fresh on the stalk, the vine and the hoof.

During prohibition our self-sufficiency went one step further. Sarah, the parlormaid, secretly set up a still in the cellar where she distilled gin and brewed beer, which she then sold surreptitiously to our friends in the neighborhood. It was not until some of Muzzy's friends congratulated her on the quality of the Kyneton gin and beer that she discovered the goings on in the cellar. Thereafter, Sarah made gin and beer for us too.

Muzzy seldom served hard drinks to her tennis guests. There was hot tea and ice tea and something called raspberry vinegar—a syrupy homemade concoction that, mixed with water, we thought was delicious. There was never any Coca-Cola. Muzzy had been told it contained dope and forbade us to drink it.

While Muzzy served tea, Lizzy fretted and worried about whether there was enough food for supper. Muzzy was too preoccupied to give the matter any thought until the tea and the raspberry vinegar were cleared away. Only then she made a vague head count and sent a tentative estimate to "the back." There would be twelve or fourteen or perhaps fifteen for supper—probably. Lizzy sighed at the news. She figured she could just make the food stretch to fifteen—but no more. Half an hour later another check brought the estimate down to thirteen and then a few minutes later up to seventeen. Lizzy moaned. Sarah, who was the Bolshevik of "the back," needled her:

"Why don't you tell the Madam there ain't enough?"

"It's my business to see there is enough," the loyal Lizzy retorted and went to the kitchen door to call John, who was smoking his Sunday pipe placidly in the stable yard. She told him to pluck another chicken and pick another quart of peas. Calmly, unaware of the crisis in "the back," Muzzy continued to chat with her guests. When finally we all swarmed into the dining room and Muzzy began seating her guests, she discovered that one mouth had somehow been overlooked. Chagrined, she sent the bad news to Lizzy and had one of us squeeze in one more place.

"Poor Liz," she sighed and made a mental note to apologize to her about the unexpected guest.

After supper the young were sent to bed and the older children and their friends gathered around the piano while Sissy, my eldest sister, played songs from a book called something like "Music for All Occasions." They sang, "Over the bannister leans a face tender and sweet and beguiling" and "Way down upon the Swanee River." In a more frivolous mood they sang, "I'm a little prairie flower growing wilder by the hour." My favorite was "Old Black Joe," the strains of which reaching me on the sleeping porch sounded so sad that I often cried myself to sleep when they sang it.

When the autumn rains put an end to tennis, Muzzy cast about for something to take its place. She hadn't far to look. Football had always been lurking in the background ever since Daddy had helped organize the first

Penn team. And now George was on the varsity football squad at Penn and our lives centered on the team.

Naturally we all trooped to Franklin Field every Saturday to watch brother George and to cheer hysterically. We even followed the team to nearby towns when they played away. Once Penn was chosen to play California at Berkeley. Uncle Walter Thayer, another fanatical fan, arranged for Muzzy and me to go with him and the squad to the West Coast. It took four days to cross the continent in a special train. Muzzy was the only female aboard.

We had hardly pulled out of Broad Street Station to the screams of the rooters left behind when members of the squad began drifting into our compartment ostensibly to chat. But before long they began bringing more than just their company. Sheepishly at first they sought Muzzy's help in performing the small chores usually done by their mothers and sisters. There were socks to darn, pants to mend, buttons to be sewn onto shirts.

As the pile of mending mounted in the compartment, Uncle Walter said angrily, "This is supposed to be a vacation for your mother. At home she spends her whole time running the family on Muzzy power. Now she's powering the whole damn football squad."

Whenever the train stopped for a few minutes at a station, the squad swarmed out onto the platform and did setting-up exercises or ran through signal practice while Muzzy watched, rolling her eyes in silent dismay whenever one of the players dashed off in the wrong direction. Nearby the Penn band practiced our campaign song, "California, Here We Come," which prophesied how we were going to slaughter the Californians. We didn't but nobody blamed Muzzy for the defeat.

Muzzy enjoyed watching football but she preferred to play it. So every Sunday during the autumn she organized a game of touch football in the cow pasture at Kyneton. Friends of George's from Penn, acquaintances from Princeton, neighbors, cousins and friends joined us. The younger children were relegated to the line but Muzzy preferred the backfield.

Touch football at Kyneton was not child's play. A touch was supposed to be the equivalent of a tackle but the fierce competition and antagonisms between players often called for more convincing proof that the runner was really caught.

One Sunday the guests included a star Princeton varsity player called Jack Strubing, who weighed a good two hundred pounds. Also among the players was a cousin of ours, Max deSchauensee, who had been brought up in Italy, where he had played nothing more violent than a violin. He was at the time a student opera singer. Awkward and ill-coordinated, he was invariably among the last to be chosen when we picked sides.

At one point Muzzy, playing against Strubing, claimed to have tagged him. Strubing denied it. We Kynetonians were scandalized at his contradicting Muzzy but Muzzy silenced us. On the next play Strubing again carried the ball. No one paid any attention as the clumsy Max charged through the line but there was blazing fury in his eyes as he hurled himself headlong at the huge Princetonian and brought him crashing to the ground in a perfect flying tackle. Max was laid up for the rest of the game but he was the hero of the day, and the next Sunday he was among the first to be chosen.

Injuries were frequent for the field itself was rough and often frozen. Besides, the cows had strewn it liberally with slippery manure. Bruised shoulders, twisted ankles and even broken bones were not unusual. Muzzy with her contempt for frailty paid little attention to these calamities except perhaps a word of sympathy when the cripples limped into the drawing room for tea after the game.

Others took the injuries seriously. After several members of the Princeton varsity squad had been laid up playing at Kyneton, the Princeton coach posted a notice on the training-house bulletin board forbidding his players from playing touch with the Thayers. We were all delighted when we heard about it, especially Muzzy. It just proved how frail Princetonians really are.

Touch went on all autumn and into the winter even when there was snow on the ground. The only thing that stopped it was when the ponds in the neighborhood froze over. Then the hockey season began. Muzzy had learned to skate as a child but she had been restricted to ladylike figure skating and could cut a sharp figure eight and even a three. So she patiently taught us the inner edge and the more difficult outer edge.

However, we considered fancy skating, as we called it, effete and sissy. When Muzzy visited me later at St. Paul's School, she always brought her figure skates. I was mortified when during breaks between classes on Saturday mornings we looked out at the main hockey rink, which had been scraped to a flawless mirror-like surface in preparation for the big game that afternoon. A slim little figure in black would be gliding over it practicing her edges and leaving ugly scars on the glistening ice. When my classmates asked who the culprit could be, I slunk off in shamed silence.

Many years later Muzzy was visiting one of her grandchildren at St. Paul's when an early frost froze over the hockey pond. Muzzy rushed to the school office and wrote out a telegram to Kyneton for her figure skates. The school secretary glanced at the telegram and then looked at Muzzy. A little hesitantly she asked Muzzy how old she was.

"Seventy-five," Muzzy snapped. "What's that got to do with it?"

At Kyneton we generally skated on a nearby pond known as "the dump" because it was used by our neighbors to dispose of old junk, iron pots, bedsprings and cans. Occasionally one of these objects would protrude from the ice and cause spectacular falls when a skate caught in it.

Bowing to our preference for hockey over figure eights, Muzzy quickly learned to play. Hockey was rougher than touch football and even Muzzy broke her wrist. In fact she broke it twice. The second time was when she was teaching her grandchildren the intricacies of body checking. By then she was a highly proficient player and could shoot a puck the length of the dump.

The day she broke her wrist for the second time, two of her grandsons, each about ten years old, were trudging sadly back up the hill to Kyneton carrying their skates. "You know," Billy Almy solemnly said to his cousin Joe Fox, "Grandmother is really a *great* puck handler."

When the snow finally covered the dump and made hockey impossible, Muzzy sent us down to the cellar to get out the sleds and the toboggan. Our sledding slope was the steep hill at the back of the property, which ended in a rock pile. Muzzy's favorite sled was the big six-man toboggan, which she loaded with children and guests, the bigger the better. Her favorite companions were two Wheeler cousins, Andrew and Alec, each of whom weighed well over two hundred and fifty pounds. Muzzy always sat in front and steered as they hurtled down the hill. The object of the game was to avoid the rock pile. Usually she did but when she didn't there were inevitably some bruised bodies and bloody heads to say nothing of a badly bent toboggan.

Muzzy was in her sixties when skiing came to America. She immediately acquired some skis and started practicing on the big hill. Eventually she became good enough to take some of us to Lake Placid, where she managed most of the runs even though she never got much beyond the stemming stage.

It was around that time that one of my sister's beaux found himself having tea alone with Muzzy. He was a pompous, tactless ass, which was probably why my sister disappeared when he called. Anxious to impress Muzzy with his wisdom and maturity, he remarked sententiously that his ambition was to perfect his skills in tennis and golf before he was forty.

"After that age," he said, "one doesn't really learn anything."

Muzzy looked at him meekly and then in her small, mild voice shot one of her poison arrows: "After I was forty I learned to cook, drive a car, ski and dive headfirst."

The one activity that I cannot recall Muzzy actively taking part in was my skunk-trapping. But even there she played an important if peripheral role.

After many years of laying traps in the woods and streams around Kyneton I finally managed one day to catch a skunk. The animal was still alive when I discovered it, and before I could kill it, my clothes were drenched with its nauseating perfume. As soon as I got home, the clothes were buried in the garden. Then I skinned the beast and announced I wanted to have a stole made of it for my old German nurse Elise.

Muzzy as usual offered to take the hide to the tanner wrapped in a newspaper. The tanner lived far up Broad Street in North Philadelphia. So Muzzy took a trolley car. The car was full when she got in but very soon she found she was riding alone with the motorman. When at last she reached her stop and started to get out, the motorman, a large red handkerchief pressed to his face, turned to her. "Lady, what in hell's name have you got in that newspaper?"

Blushing scarlet, Muzzy mumbled something about her son's skunk and leapt from the car. Elise thanked me warmly for the stole but I doubt if she wore it much. When many years later an inventory was made of Kyneton, among the items listed was "one skunk stole. Value $2.00."

Muzzy took it for granted that her four daughters should compete in every sport along with her sons and cultivate the same manliness as they. She was considerably less interested in their womanliness. While she acknowledged her obligations to them and to Philadelphia social conventions, she fulfilled her duties with the minimum of enthusiasm.

Muzzy was not unconventional. She merely assigned a rather low priority to conventions. When she was younger, she enjoyed going to the Assembly and after she was married she even served as patroness on occasion.

She tried to teach the girls to stand up straight, talk in a well-modulated voice, avoid vulgarity, including both dirty stories and rough language, and to speak without a local accent. It was provincial, she thought, to speak in a way that could be identified with any particular place—except perhaps England.

She also believed that speaking French was not an accomplishment but an obligation. From the age of six all of us were subjected each week to a French afternoon under a French mademoiselle. The results, alas, fell considerably short of her hopes. I for one was still taking French lessons twenty years later and my grammar was still atrocious and my accent worse. The rest of the family were not much better.

She also admitted that the girls at least should learn to dance properly. They were taught the rudiments at Kyneton School and then at the age of fourteen or so were enrolled in Mr. Asher's dancing class in town. Later they went to the Friday Evening, where they actually danced with boys, and the next year finished off at the Saturday Evening, where they learned the art of getting cut in on or, failing that, being a wallflower without panicking. At the Saturday Evening they also learned to sit out with partners in corners discreetly enough to avoid censure from the watchful eyes of parents but alluringly enough to please the boys. Kissing under the staircase was forbidden and even holding hands was heavily frowned upon.

Invitations to the Saturday Evening were presided over by a committee of parents who kept a critical eye on the lists to exclude undesirables or girls they considered too young for such affairs. When my sister Betsy's best friend added a fictitious year to her age so she could attend, Muzzy found out about it and after an agonizing reappraisal of the girl's invitation withdrew it.

George and I too were forced to go to dancing class at Asher's. We both loathed it, as it constantly interfered with George's football practice or my skunk-trapping. Personally, I learned little or nothing at Asher's and when I eventually entered West Point, I spent the first hot summer at dancing class, waltzing with other sweating plebes. But it was not all Mr. Asher's fault. My sense of rhythm had something to do with it. Muzzy used to say she could always spot me when I was parading with the 1,200-strong cadet corps. She said my head always popped up just when the other 1,199 were going down.

Muzzy also recognized the necessity of "bringing out" her daughters and introducing them as débutantes to society. Some ambitious parents gave lavish balls at the Ritz or the Bellevue for their daughters but Muzzy considered this far beyond her means—or at least far beyond what the bank allowed her to spend and anyway a bit on the ostentatious side. So she confined herself to a tea each for the four girls—at Kyneton. Sticking to older conventions, she did not invite other young girls or boys to these affairs but only her friends to whom in theory she was introducing her young for the first time.

The coming-out teas were very formal. There were extra waitresses to pass the sandwiches and tables were set up around the garden in the hope it would not rain. Augustus stood at the front door, with a clean white shirt and wing collar, and shook hands with the old family friends as they entered and then formally announced them. I usually sat in a window on the third floor looking down at the guests in the garden and wondering why in the world they had come at all.

The biggest event for the girls was their first Assembly. The Philadelphia Assembly was a subscription ball with a somewhat limited invitation list. Rules for admission were strict. Divorcées might go but divorcées who remarried were excluded. Invitations were eagerly sought by new families in Philadelphia whether their arrival was financial or merely geographical. Their social arrival depended on whether they got an invitation or not. Occasionally overambitious new parents were not above offering substantial bribes to the invitation committee. But it was unfortunately also true that some overzealous members of the committee were known to demand large contributions to their favorite charities before they admitted the contributors' daughters.

The ball itself was always at the Bellevue, the ladies in long dresses and the men in white tie and tails. Going through the receiving line, the ladies had to make full curtsies to the half-dozen patronesses. The gentlemen bowed from the waist. Once when I invited a fellow-West Point cadet who came from Texas to the ball, he took one look at the struggling ladies at the receiving line and remarked that they looked like rheumatic Shorthorns trying to get up.

Supper always included Philadelphia terrapin, which according to rumor was sometimes made from rats when turtles were in short supply.

Muzzy liked pretty clothes and, when she was young, enjoyed nothing better than browsing through the shops of Paris and Rome and attending fashion shows. She said she inherited her frivolous taste from her grandmother, known as Little Granny. Little Granny had a passion for gay hats but as a Quaker she was allowed to wear only gray bonnets. Whenever she accompanied the Wheelers to Europe, she spent her days in the milliners' shops picking out the raciest gray bonnets she could find on the Continent.

But after Daddy died, Muzzy seldom bought herself new dresses. There were too many other things to buy with the money the bank allowed her. There was always enough for footballs and hockey sticks and tennis rackets for the boys, but as for "coming out" dresses the girls had to make do with the creations of Bridget Arkwright.

Every year Bridget, the seamstress, made the rounds of the homes of Muzzy and her friends, spending a few weeks in each. She let out hems, tucked up shirtwaists, repaired ball dresses and otherwise rehabilitated the family wardrobe. Then she moved on to the next household. Her tastes had been formed in the nineties and her styles never quite caught up with the Paris fashions, models of which were already appearing in Philadelphia's better stores.

Little by little other parents began to discover the French models and buy them for their children. But to the disappointment of my sisters Muzzy considered Bridget quite adequate in the circumstances. Possibly her greatest triumph was the three-in-one creation for Buckety's coming-out season. It consisted of a long silver lamé sheath over which could be draped any one of three transparent chiffon garments of different colors. Thus, she pointed out exultantly, by simply alternating the chiffon Buckety had a different dress for every party. Buckety never saw it quite that way. As Bridget grew older, and her creations dropped farther and farther behind her competition in Paris, her clients one by one dropped away. So one day she arrived for her annual tour at Kyneton and stayed for the rest of her life.

She was not the only one. My sisters used to complain sourly that Kyneton was like the place in Africa where old elephants went to die. Augustus, for example, must have been nearly a hundred years old when he took sick for the last time in the jam closet in the cellar. And there was Margaret, John Nagle's sister, who also began her career at Pembroke and later went on to work in the more elegant homes of various aunts and uncles. She was a big clumsy woman and as she grew feebler she too was put out to pasture at Kyneton. Margaret was not always able to conceal her disdain for the plain atmosphere of Kyneton and Muzzy retaliated by gently but firmly pointing out Margaret's own imperfections. Once Margaret dropped a jam pot on the rug and knelt down to wipe up the mess. Suddenly she seemed to lose her balance and fell over.

Muzzy tried to conceal her impatience with her awkwardness. "Really, Maggie," she began. But Margaret had had a heart attack and wiping up the jam was her last chore.

It was the same with all the servants. There was Louise, who finally retired at the age of seventy-five after thirty-one years at Kyneton. And there was Sarah, who made moonshine in the cellar, and her daughter, Mary Elizabeth, who lived with her in "the back." Mary Elizabeth, who was Avis's age, spent most of her time in "the front" playing with the rest of us. But sometimes when there was a large party, she helped serve at dinner. One night Muzzy was presiding over a formal dinner and trying to achieve the elegant standards of Pembroke with its butlers and footmen. After the first course was finished, she whispered to Mary Elizabeth to pass the oyster bisque again.

"There ain't no more oysters, Muz," Mary Elizabeth said loudly. "Just that milky soup."

When Sarah finally retired after twenty-seven years, Mary Elizabeth to our great distress went with her, the only person to leave Kyneton's "back" before she reached seventy.

But Bridget looked, at least, the oldest of them all. She was a minute woman with badly fitting false teeth usually concealed behind tightly pressed lips that bristled with pins. When she was not pedaling on the sewing machine, she was usually brushing her long silvery hair. She smelt of old damp wool and she was stone deaf. She also liked gin.

The sewing room, where she lived and worked, was on the third floor next to the boys' dormitory. She was supposed to use the bathroom in "the back" but mostly she used ours. Like all other doors at Kyneton, the one in the bathroom had no proper lock and Bridget was forever bursting in on us, deaf to our protests as we hid naked behind the shower curtain. We got accustomed to her interruptions but not all our friends did.

One night a beau of Betsy's was sitting with her in the drawing room having a nightcap after a dance. As they discussed the evening, he suddenly stopped, his mouth agape, his eyes staring horrified at the large mirror in the hall. Betsy looked at the mirror and there dimly reflected she saw a tiny little gnome in a purple dressing gown trotting nimbly down the stairs, silver hair flowing behind. The withered face was wreathed in a sly, toothless smile and the eyes gleamed mischievously. The gnome made straight for the moosehead, climbed on the chair beneath it and, reaching into its nostril, took out the key to the liquor closet. Opening it stealthily, she reached for the gin bottle and, as Betsy and her friend stared in fascination, took several healthy swigs. Then, replacing the bottle, the gnome silently flitted back up the stairs.

The beau turned to Betsy questioningly. But Betsy was not one to sully the good name of Kyneton with revelations about drunken seamstresses.

"I thought Laura's dress was very becoming, this evening, didn't you?" she said blithely, hoping her beau would forget the whole thing or dismiss it as a hallucination. But when it came time for the beau to go to bed up in the boys' dormitory, he suddenly remembered he was expected elsewhere and left Kyneton forever.

Bridget Arkwright was not the only obstacle my sisters faced when they entertained their beaux at Kyneton. There was the grandfather clock, which after Daddy's death Muzzy wound vigorously each Sunday morning—sometimes a little too vigorously. My sister Buckety at that time had a beau whom we all liked immensely. One night after taking Buckety to a dance, he was invited to spend the night in the dormitory.

When he got to bed, he wondered how late it was. Far off he could hear the old grandfather clock booming the hour. He counted the strokes drowsily. But when the clock struck thirteen, he started, wide awake. As it boomed on, his muscles tensed and the hair on his neck bristled. He had counted to a hundred and twenty-three when the clock suddenly fell silent. He rose, dressed, and fled from Kyneton's weird atmosphere. However, he soon recovered and eventually became my brother-in-law.

EIGHT

Pocono

IN SUMMER the Main Line with its torrid humidity was not fit for human habitation—or at least not for Muzzy's children she decided, just as her father had decided earlier when he took his family to Newport. But Newport, the trustees decreed, was far too chic and expensive for her tastes and budget. Many Philadelphians had adopted Mount Desert Island, where in Bar Harbor and Northeast they had built summer homes. Every night from July to September the Bar Harbor express carried entire clans of Philadelphians complete with servants and nurses direct to Mount Desert Island.

But to transport herself and six children by Pullman to Mount Desert was also more than Muzzy's trustees would allow her. Besides while Daddy was alive, it would have been impossible for him to spend even the weekend with us. So they settled on Pocono Lake Preserve, a private reservation run by a group of Philadelphia Quakers headed by the Carey family, in the Pocono Mountains less than a hundred miles from Philadelphia. There at least Daddy could come up on weekends in the Buick supplied by the shipyard. The Buick had a self-starter.

The rest of us made the annual trek in the Ford. Preparations for the journey began days in advance—at least for me. Though I was one of the youngest, I had appointed myself chief transportation officer of the family, perhaps because of my experience motoring home from Oklahoma with Muzzy and Daddy. But the others said it was simply my Caesar complex asserting itself. Anyway, two or three days before we were to start, I packed my toothbrush to relieve myself of one burdensome chore during the hectic days ahead. Then I packed my personal equipment—traps, fishing rods and camping gear. Finally I strapped my hunting knife, my compass and my canteen to my belt. My sisters objected strenuously to the canteen because it always bored into the buttocks of whomever I sat beside in the car. But I had learned from reading about Daniel Boone and watching William S. Hart that only a greenhorn would be separated from his emergency water supply on the long and dangerous journey that lay before us.

Since the cottage we rented was equipped for about half as many people as Muzzy usually took with her, we had to take extra cots, blankets, towels and even tents. There must have been some way of shipping these ahead by train but Muzzy considered that unsporting. So the day before take-off the Ford was parked at the front door and racks fastened to the running boards. The racks made it impossible to open the doors but Muzzy soon learned to take the doors literally in her stride.

All day and late into the evening I stowed the pile of equipment till the springs, even without the passengers, were almost flat. The girls complained that I never left enough room for them. I might have pointed out that the Ford was no Greyhound bus but I was much too busy lashing down a pile of pillows on the folded-back top. We never would have found room for everything if we had put the top up so we just took our chances with the weather—and occasionally lost, cowering low under our hats as the rain swept over us. It was just bad luck, Muzzy would explain when it rained, and we knew we were not allowed to complain of bad luck.

As zero hour approached, Kyneton rose to a frenzy of activity. Everyone remembered some last-minute necessity, which I then in a fury had to find a place for. Often it was the picnic basket or a dog. At last after giving final instructions to the servants Muzzy appeared. She was clad in khaki riding breeches from the Army & Navy Store, which laced up to the knee so that she could leap in and out over the baggage on the running board.

Avis and I scrambled over the barriers of baggage into our seats beside Muzzy. The rest squeezed in behind.

Our course lay north by northwest along the Delaware River through the Wind Gap and the Water Gap. Today a six-lane highway leads direct to the Poconos.

The routes are all numbered and signs warn you where to turn several miles ahead so you have time to slow down. In those days the roads had names and there were few directions signs and no turn-off warnings. But I have always preferred names to numbers and Muzzy needed only a few yards to slow down for a turn.

There were practically no road maps in those days and we relied exclusively on the *Blue Book* for navigation. The *Blue Book* was a large volume that we got through the Automobile Club describing in detail how to get from one town to another. Once you knew where you were and had decided on your next objective, the *Blue Book* guided you step by step, turn by turn and sometimes, but not always, fork by fork. It told us to turn right at the red brick schoolhouse at Good Hope and sharp left at the yellow firehouse a mile or two out of town and then right at the fork at Mill Road, straight through Millville to the cemetery, where you jogged left. We never agreed on what "jogging left" meant. Some of us argued that it meant turning right and then sharp left and the others maintained it was the other way around. So whenever we came to a jog in the *Blue Book,* there was a noisy argument among us. Muzzy, trying to be scrupulously fair and impartial, decided half the time for one school of thought, the other half for the other.

As long as you kept careful track of where you were and followed the instructions, "you couldn't miss it" as the saying went. But the *Blue Book* itself appeared only every few years while the landmarks it relied on did not always remain the same. Sometimes the schoolhouse had burned down, the firehouse had been repainted gray, the fork had become a crossroad or the road through Millville was under repairs calling for a two-mile unmarked detour. Success therefore depended largely on memories of last year, intuition, imagination and considerable good luck.

The entire family, of course, participated in every debate on where or which way to turn or not to turn—all except Sissy, who usually brooded in silence, probably composing poetry.

"I remember this place!" Betsy screamed. "It's where Iota was sick. We go left."

"The book says . . . ," I pointed out, reading from the directions.

"We went wrong here last time," Buckety murmured gloomily and Avis agreed. In the end Muzzy, frowning anxiously, made the decision.

When we made the wrong turn, it often took some time to discover our mistake as we tried to fit the topography of the wrong road to the directions in the *Blue Book.*

"Left at the fork by the giant oak," I read from the book.

"There's the oak," Betsy said, pointing to a tree ahead.

"It's a chestnut," Buckety muttered. It was Betsy's turn to be right, Muzzy decided, so we turned and went whizzing down a dirt road.

"Half a mile, turn right at top of hill," I read from the book.

For several miles there was not the slightest sign of a hill and the girls began to glare angrily at me as though I were making it all up. Eventually there was a slight rise, and a little farther on another road went off to the right. After a long discussion we took it. Then suddenly we were confronted by a fork. There was nothing about the fork in the book and again the girls glared at me. We took the most traveled branch but within a mile it dwindled to a muddy lane and crossed a deep creek by a ford.

Muzzy looked doubtfully at the ford but then, making up her mind, she jerked down the gas lever and we charged ahead. The water lapped the sides, soaking the baggage in the racks. The motor stuttered. Avis began to whimper but in a final surge of life the car crawled to the opposite bank before the engine died.

We waited until the spark plugs or distributor or whatever it was dried, then, cranking in turns, we got the motor running again and pushed on through a deep wood. The track led to a dilapidated old shack with a large stovepipe sticking through the roof, making it look like a moonshiner's still. Now we all agreed we had taken a wrong turn somewhere but none of us agreed where. Muzzy hastily backed and filled in the underbrush until we got the car turned around, fearful that any moment the moonshiner would appear with a shotgun and blow our heads off.

We retraced our steps, charged once more across the creek and eventually reached the giant oak, which Muzzy identified as a walnut.

Only as a last extremity would Muzzy consider asking directions from passersby. She thought it was cheating. But now as we stood ruefully under the walnut, she knew we were beaten. Still, before she asked for help, she was going to select our rescuer carefully.

Another car came by and stopped. At the wheel was an unshaven farmer. Beside him a girl was sitting—a little too close to him to suit Muzzy. So she waved them on. We children, considering ourselves worse than shipwrecked on a desert island, wailed in protest as the car drove off.

"But they're not very nice people," Muzzy explained defensively.

A half hour went by and finally another ancient Ford came along and stopped. At the wheel sat a bearded man with a wide felt hat, obviously a local Mennonite. Muzzy practically threw herself on him for she dearly loved the God-fearing Mennonites. "So clean and wholesome," she said.

Acting as though she were a refugee fleeing with her brood before an invading army, she told him the story of the wrong tree. The man looked at her for several moments speechless.

"Vere you vant to go?" he finally asked. Hearing the strange accent, Buckety doubled up. Betsy's shoulders heaved as she tried desperately to suppress her giggles. Sissy held out just a second longer and then the whole car rocked as we giggled uncontrollably. Muzzy bit her lip and managed to murmur, "Water Gap."

"Vasser Gap data vay," the man said, pointing in the

direction we had originally come from. Then he drove on, leaving all of us convulsed in laughter.

Sometimes it was even worse. It was remarkable how often we asked the way of a deaf-mute, a stutterer or the village idiot. Then even Muzzy broke down in helpless giggles and afterward scolded herself and us unmercifully for our bad manners.

It was hardly noon when murmurs from the back seat indicated that its occupants were getting hungry so we all started looking for an ideal picnic ground. Sissy suggested a high hill with a spectacular view but I at once vetoed it because there was no water. Betsy proposed a lush meadow but it turned out to be a swamp. As we drove on proposing and rejecting, the pangs of hunger grew sharper. At last we all agreed to stop under the first tree and eat by the roadside, chewing our sandwiches sprinkled with the dust of other cars.

Today one speeds along at seventy or eighty and makes the journey to Pocono in a couple of hours, but I am sure our trips were infinitely more instructive and exciting if not so quick or comfortable. Aside from the satisfaction of eventually reaching Millville or the Water Gap and finally Pocono, there were the unexpected distractions like potholes that blew out our tires, concealed ditches that broke our springs and detours on muddy lanes that would have been a challenge to a modern tank.

I had carefully figured that if we managed to average twenty miles an hour we could make the trip in daylight. But we seldom arrived at our cottage till well after dark. Then Muzzy would quickly take an aspirin to stifle her headache while the rest of us lit oil lamps and barged about arguing where each of us would sleep.

I generally took my tent out into the woods and pitched it in the dark, making a hasty bed of balsam boughs. During the night I usually discovered, to the delight of my sisters, that I had made the bed directly over an anthill.

George generally managed to avoid the annual trek either because he was off vacationing with friends or later because he was at summer football training. Once when he did come to Pocono, he was cranking the Ford when it kicked back and broke his arm. As he hopped about holding his wrist and shouting in agony, the rest of us, especially Muzzy, were thrown into despair, not because his arm hurt but because it might interfere with his football career.

Summers at Pocono consisted chiefly of long days of swimming or fishing minute perch off the dock at the foot of the cottage, or picking blueberries in the woods behind it, or decorating our rowboat to take part in the annual water carnival organized by the Careys.

Sissy generally designed our carnival entry while the rest of us sweated with the scenery. Her best effort was converting the rowboat into a woodland bower in which a Fairy Princess (Sissy) and Prince Charming (Buckety) reclined discreetly. The crew consisted of Betsy and me with paddles fore and aft. All one week we collected moss to cover the boat and boughs of balsam and fir and birch trees and flowers. Sissy was veiled in gauze bandages and Buckety wore Muzzy's riding breeches. We were very proud of the final effect and Muzzy was sure we would win the contest. But as ours was practically the only boat without at least an outboard motor we were relegated to the end of the flotilla and by the time we passed the judges' boat it was pitch dark and all the judges could see was a dark shadow splashing forlornly through the water.

The winners that year were a family called Colgate, who owned a large motorboat on which a minstrel quartet sang what may have been the first singing commercial:

> "Colgate Ribbon Dental Cream!
> Comes out like a ribbon,
> Lies flat on the brush,
> Colgate Ribbon Dental Cream!"

Muzzy thought the song was just a trifle on the vulgar side.

There were calamities too to break the routine and provide topics of conversation for the winter months ahead: the all-night search for the old lady who got lost in the woods looking for berries; the rusty nail I stepped on while building a raft, which laid me up for most of a summer; the two boys who went over the dam at the foot of the lake in a canoe. The dam was only about ten feet high but to us it was Niagara and the fact that the boys were not hurt was, we decided, a miracle.

But for Muzzy probably the greatest event in all our years at Pocono was learning to dive headfirst. George already knew how to dive and undertook to teach my sisters and me. Watching us bent over the edge of the dock staring terrified into the deep water while George held our ankles, Muzzy decided that she too must learn. So we all took turns holding Muzzy's black-stockinged ankles as she bent double, her head swathed in a ruffled black bathing cap, her fingers laced over her head. For the first week or so as she swayed forward, she managed to kick free her ankles at the last moment and drop into the water like a hairpin. But gradually she learned to overcome her fears and toppled into the water with her hands just ahead of her feet. Eventually she became quite adept and could plunge elegantly into the lake, her black skirts billowing behind her.

But as we grew older, Pocono's Quaker calm began to pall and one by one we took to spending our summers with friends at Northeast or Bar Harbor. In the end Muzzy gave up the cottage and took those who were left farther afield. For several years we visited our cousins, the Packards, who had a large camp on Upper Saranac Lake in the Adirondacks. There we had motorboats, guide boats for camping trips and even pickerel in place of the tiny perch at Pocono.

The journey to Saranac was, however, far longer than to Pocono and Muzzy finally persuaded the trustees to let her buy a Dodge. It was, of course, a touring car. Muzzy had to have her fresh air and besides, she said, closed cars were drafty. And the Dodge did have a self-starter, which worked whenever the battery was not run down.

Even with the Dodge it generally took us two days and sometimes longer to cover the three-hundred-mile stretch. The Packards always went by train and thought Muzzy was a little odd to try it by car. But she said there was no fun in trains. They almost always got there and usually on time. With a car, in contrast, there was a large and exciting element of sporting chance. It was not quite like touch football but it was still a game.

Broken springs, overheated engines and flat tires were routine. Muzzy became a competent tire changer and in a pinch could patch an inner tube. But the day the rear end fell out she was definitely beyond her depth.

For some reason Sissy was with us on that trip and was driving as we approached Glens Falls. Glens Falls had always been a mine field of troubles for us and the closer we got the tenser we all became. What had it in store for us this time?

Perhaps it was because Sissy's nerves were on edge or perhaps it was because she had not quite mastered the clutch and gearshift with three speeds. But whatever it was, when we came to a deep ditch across the road, she pushed the wrong pedal and the car leapt forward, the front wheels clearing the ditch nicely like a well-trained jumper. But the rear wheels fell short and crashed into the ditch. There was a fearful grinding of cogwheels as the Dodge came to a halt.

Muzzy bit her lip. Sissy began to cry. Avis wailed and I started scolding. We piled out and peered ignorantly under the rear of the car whence the death rattle had come but we saw nothing wrong.

It began to rain. We wrestled the top up into place

and Muzzy ordered us to get in and wait. Dressed as usual in her khaki riding breeches, she stood in the road and waited for someone to come by. Eventually a truck stopped and the driver, peering beneath the Dodge, announced that the rear end had fallen out. There was nothing on the road behind us resembling what might be called a rear end but anyway we accepted the driver's word. Muzzy and the girls climbed into the back of the truck and departed while I waited for a wrecker, since the Dodge was beyond being towed.

In Glens Falls, Muzzy spurned the little commercial hotel and the regular boarding houses were all full, but eventually on a back street she found a "TOURISTS ACCOMMODATED" sign and a kindly housewife who agreed to put us up for what we told her would be one night. At the garage we were informed that the differential and the drive-shaft housing were beyond repair. Spare parts would have to be sent from the factory.

We fretted and whiled away the time by walking around the little town. Glens Falls was not much of a tourist attraction in those days and we wandered up and down the Main Street, pausing frequently at the garage for bulletins on the state of the Dodge. Eventually the spare parts arrived, the car was put in order and we were about to set off again for Saranac when another serious crisis arose.

Muzzy's money belt, we discovered, contained less than ten dollars.

"I can't imagine why I didn't cash a check before we left," she muttered to herself. She persuaded the landlady to take a check but the garage owner was less accommodating until Muzzy, fumbling in her purse, pulled out her visiting card, which read simply "Mrs. George C. Thayer." With a flourish she handed it to the garageman. He was so taken aback at this novel way of establishing her credit rating that he took her check without a murmur.

So at last we piled the baggage back into the Dodge and set off for Saranac three days behind schedule. I still have a photo of the landlady, a look of profound relief on her face as she waved us on our way.

Our longest expedition was to Mount Desert Island, which we finally reached after a four-day trip in the Dodge. Muzzy had rented the butler's cottage on a big summer estate in the southwestern corner of the island. It was obviously the wrong corner for no one else ever came there. Even my sister Betsy, now a débutante, found it so unchic that she never came near us but stayed with friends in fashionable Northeast Harbor.

The cottage itself consisted of two rooms. Muzzy and the girls slept on cots or mattresses in the back room, George and I on the floor of the kitchen.

Buckety, who was then engaged, spent her time mooning about the coves and inlets. Avis picked wild flowers by the fistful. I tried to catch the seals who sunbathed on rocks off the shore but eventually satisfied myself with photographing them. Muzzy cooked, made beds, washed, cleaned up and regularly went swimming in the bitterly cold water, diving headfirst among the rocks so as not to lose the knack so painfully acquired at Pocono.

NINE

Travel That Broadened

ONE SPRING Muzzy decided it was high time we all went abroad and got cultured. She broached the subject to the bank with such enthusiasm that to our amazement it gave in and provided Muzzy not only with tickets but with a letter of credit, which she tucked away in the money belt under her skirt. Friends had urged her to take traveler's checks because they were much more convenient. But Muzzy insisted on a letter of credit. That was the way it had always been done when she was a child.

To be sure none of us was bored, each of us was allowed to invite a friend along. I asked a schoolmate from St. Paul's. George brought Zip Long, a football friend from Penn. Fortunately we traveled in shifts. Sissy and Buckety were married and stayed behind. Betsy was already in Paris at a finishing school so Muzzy and Avis went as the advance guard traveling

Second Class. Muzzy said she preferred traveling Second Class because you always met such interesting English people in Second. Our English cousins objected vigorously to the implications of this explanation.

George and I and our friends traveled Student Third Class on an ancient Holland American Line ship that took eleven days for the crossing. All but one of those days I spent with German measles in the ship's Third Class hospital, located in a deckhouse overlooking the tiny Student Third deck on which hundreds of college boys and girls milled about day and night.

It was my first exposure to the gilded youth of the roaring twenties and the sights I saw at night from my porthole shook me far worse than the German measles. I trembled with anxiety for the virtue of my brother and our friends as I watched the carousing beer-drinking mob strolling along with arms around each other and sometimes even kissing each other. Kyneton with all its teeming hordes of guests was never like that.

George also professed to be shocked and sternly warned Zip Long not to mingle with the other passengers. But as soon as he himself had appropriated one of the prettiest girls on the boat, he relented and told Zip he too could associate with our fellow-passengers. Zip found it a little late in the game.

While my memories of the view from my deckhouse porthole on that first transatlantic crossing are still vivid, the rest of the trip and those that followed are much more spotty and, I fear, fell short of Muzzy's hopes for my cultural development.

In London, I found out that a young South Carolina girl, a friend of Betsy's whom I greatly admired, was staying in a nearby hotel. As I had until then shown interest only in birds, muskrats and skunks, Muzzy was delighted at this first sign of sociability and persuaded me to ask the young lady out for an evening on the town. I asked where I should take her and Muzzy answered, "Prince's of course. Everyone dines at Prince's."

I called Prince's and reserved a table. Then Muzzy insisted I send flowers to the girl. I protested that I didn't have enough money so she lent me a pound.

When I picked the girl up to take her to Prince's, she asked me what in the world the flowers were for and I mumbled something about Muzzy's insisting.

Muzzy was waiting anxiously when I finally returned, somewhat earlier than she had expected. She asked how it had been at Prince's. I said I guessed it was all right.

"Was it crowded as usual?" she asked.

"We were the only people there," I told her.

"Did you dance?"

I said there was no music.

A sad, nostalgic look came into Muzzy's eyes. "That's strange. It was always so gay when I was a girl."

I was gallant enough not to remind her that that was nearly forty years before. The rest of my stay in London I spent at the Regent's Park Zoo.

When we had done London, Muzzy drove us to Scotland in a rented car. She had never paid much attention to which side of the road she drove on so the left-hand driving in England didn't bother her though it occasionally resulted in a nicked fender.

With my friend I climbed Ben Nevis. When we got to the top, it was shrouded in deep fog. It seemed to me a rather puny mountain compared to the Adirondacks, especially after all I had heard about it at Kyneton School.

We spent a rainy week on the Isle of Skye and then went to Ireland, where we spent most of our time at the Dublin Horse Show.

But for all her devotion to the British Isles, Muzzy also took us to the Continent—with considerable trepidation because the French, as she constantly warned us, were not at all like the English.

We arrived in Paris during one of the worst postwar inflations and Muzzy was delighted with the number of francs she got at the Morgan Harjes Bank on her letter of credit. But it did not occur to her that if the franc was cheap to her, it might also be cheap to a Frenchman. So when she grandly tipped the first taxi driver a few centimes, she was stunned when he leapt up and down on the sidewalk, tossed the coins in the gutter and spat after them shrieking wildly. Taxi drivers had never done that in her day. But she got the idea and raised her tipping rate accordingly.

With nearly a dozen children to bed down, Muzzy was understandably economical when it came to choosing a hotel. But I would still like to know who ever recommended the Hotel Roosevelt on Avenue d'Iena. It was a small, smelly establishment with one antediluvian bathtub on each floor. Recalling now some of the other occupants, I daresay it also rented rooms by the hour.

Muzzy occupied a wedge-shaped room equipped with a washbasin and a bidet, an object none of us children had ever seen before. Muzzy used it to keep the breakfast eggs in. She found the extra charge for eggs at breakfast so exorbitant that she bought them in the market and cooked them herself on a Sterno stove.

When we asked Muzzy what the bidet was for, she blushed, looked vaguer than usual and stammered, "It's for—it's—well—I use it to keep the eggs in," she finally blurted out. We eventually found out what it was for but not from Muzzy.

The Hotel Roosevelt has long since folded but the building still stands across the street from the American Ambassador's Residence. Nowadays when I visit my sister at the Residence, I occasionally give in to some masochistic urge and go across the street to revive my memories of that dreadful old hotel.

All day long Muzzy led us on the rounds of the museums of Paris at a fast trot and occasionally took us to the opera at night. She even took us once to Au Caneton for a feast of caviar and pressed duck, sighing all through the meal at the thought of trying to teach Lizzy to cook like that.

George and Zip to my dismay usually slipped off as we headed home at night to the hotel. They had found several American friends in Paris and with them, I strongly suspected, they indulged in all the wicked immoralities Paris was notorious for. Once or twice to my utter horror and disapproval Betsy went with them. But Muzzy, with what I considered incredible indifference, merely smiled when they took off.

My worst fears were confirmed when one morning we discovered George had not come home at all. Zip was deep in sleep and when we finally aroused him he told us, bleary-eyed and ashen, that the last he had seen of George he was being shoved into a police wagon. When he had revived a bit, he explained that late the night before the two of them and some other Americans had discovered a new sport consisting of jumping on Paris lampposts and bending them down to the ground. They had already doubled over half a dozen when they were surprised by a police squad. Thanks only to Zip's ability as a base runner, he had escaped from keeping the others company in the Black Maria.

Pale and silent, Muzzy and I took a taxi to Morgan Harjes, where in the privacy of an inner office Muzzy revealed to one of the vice-presidents the awful news that her eldest son was in jail. The man seemed very casual about it, as though he dealt with such calamities every day. He sent Muzzy home to the hotel and, after a phone call or two, went with me to the jail where he had located George. There he signed some papers and a few minutes later George and his friends emerged grinning sheepishly, tieless and beltless, holding up their trousers with their hands.

When we all finally reassembled and sat down to lunch, George was looking rather seedy. After a long silence Muzzy finally turned to him:

"Whatever did you do to Zip?" she asked. "He was so worried when we woke him."

When at last we had done with iniquitous Paris, Muzzy took us to the château country. As usual we went by car and as usual she rented two vehicles, both just a little too small for the number of passengers. One of them was driven by a surly young chauffeur whom Muzzy greatly admired because his French was so good.

After we had seen and photographed every château in the Loire Valley, we headed east to the Alps, our destination Venice. It was a journey no member of the family will ever forget no matter how hard we try.

As the first high mountains loomed in the distance, Muzzy's spirits rose and when we twisted and slid over the first passes she was in ecstasy. Here at last was some real sport. Whenever we encountered an onrushing car at a sharp blind hairpin turn, or slithered along the outside soft edge of the road, a thousand-foot precipice directly below, her eyes flashed with joy. When the overheated motor gave out on a steep slope and the car began to slide backward, she jumped out cheerfully and gaily put stones under the wheels. And when the brakes began to slip as we hurtled down the other side, she said with a chortle, "Merciful patience! Isn't it thrilling?" From then on whenever she spied a precarious pass on the map, she told the chauffeur to head for it.

Unfortunately none of us shared her enthusiasm for passes. Our faith in both the cars and the chauffeur was minimal and our stomachs turned whenever we peered down over a bottomless gorge. When finally we coasted down to the Italian plain, our nerves were shattered and the atmosphere in both overcrowded cars was sullen.

But we quickly recovered in Venice and were at peace again as we rode around the canals in gondolas—until Muzzy ran out of money to pay a gondolier. She was standing on the steps of San Marco when it happened. Before we could form a screen around her, she hoisted her skirt and fumbled for her money belt. The gondolier grinned. Even St. Theodore and the lion seemed to be leering down from their high pedestals and all of us blushed scarlet with shame and consternation. But Muzzy was just annoyed at our squeamishness.

"I've a perfectly good petticoat on," she said scornfully.

But the worst was when we went to the Lido and I saw for the first time men swimming without tops to their bathing suits. Even Muzzy found this a bit extreme and George was furious that she wouldn't let him take his top off too. It was clear to me that unless we got back to Kyneton soon, George was doomed to moral perdition.

At last we started back, the two cars now crammed with bulky parcels of Venetian glassware Muzzy had acquired as coming-home presents. Besides we were all a bit tired of motoring and sick to death of passes—all except Muzzy. We managed to get over the worst ones successfully by simply shutting our eyes. After the last of them we were congratulating ourselves for having escaped death by rolling over precipices when Muzzy, sharp-eyed as ever, espied another pass on the map only a few miles off our route. Without consulting the occupants of the car that followed us, she told the chauffeur to head for it. Those with her protested loudly but she insisted. "Hannibal probably crossed it with elephants," she said to me, hoping I with my animal-loving nature would be moved by the thought.

But I was not. Nor apparently were the second car's occupants. There were loud blasts on the horn behind us and the second car pulled up and stopped. Muzzy frowned as she got out and went back to see what was wrong. What she discovered was no less than open revolt. Betsy, George and their friends had had all the passes they could take and flatly refused to go on.

Muzzy was flabbergasted for it was the first time we had rebelled on the whole trip. Tense and determined, she tried to persuade them but they were adamant. Finally she called for a vote. One by one we all voted against the pass. Grimly she got back in her car and ordered the driver to turn around. The rest of the day we drove in glum silence. That evening as we sat at dinner, no one spoke. Finally Muzzy broke the dreadful silence:

"I never thought my own children would balk at a little pass."

At that point I think every one of us would gladly have gone back and crossed the pass, just to mollify Muzzy.

But she soon recovered when we reached Paris and by the time we sailed into New York Harbor she was in top form for now came the biggest game of all—going through customs.

Muzzy had nothing basic against customs. She was

not particularly for low tariffs. In fact I doubt if she ever considered the question in that light. Nor was she interested in smuggling as a money-saving device. To her smuggling was another game—a very exciting one for the stakes, she knew, were high. And at every opportunity she played it with zest.

Once returning from Europe she was met by a new son-in-law. She threw her arms around him to his amazement, for she was not one to demonstrate affection in public. Then he felt her stuff something in his pocket as she whispered in his ear, "It's a watch I haven't declared."

When they finally got through customs, Muzzy was elated at the success of her strategem. Only later did she admit that the watch was made in America and not subject to duty at all. "I just wanted to show them," she said.

Prohibition added enormously to Muzzy's sport. Once returning from South America she had hidden no less than twenty small bottles of liqueurs among her underwear. The customs inspector discovered every last one, fined her heavily and confiscated all of them. But Muzzy was not a bit dismayed when she got home. After she unpacked, she proudly displayed ten of the twenty bottles. We asked her how she had managed that.

"Perfectly simple," she said. "While the silly customs man was busy adding up my fines, I simply stuffed as many bottles as I could back in my bags."

Muzzy was not particular about whose customs she hoodwinked. French, British, German or American, they were all on the same side—against her. After World War II when England was short of food, especially imported fruits, Muzzy assumed that the lack of oranges was due to the customs' prohibiting their importation. So on her first postwar trip to England she carefully concealed dozens of oranges among her clothing. She was a little disappointed when the British inspector who found them did not confiscate them but seemed downright pleased that she was bringing them in. That wasn't the way she had been taught to play the game.

And now, returning from our grand European tour, she was planning a master stroke. She had bought no less than six large bottles of whisky, which she proposed to stuff in her overcoat pockets. But as we approached customs, warnings came back that the inspectors were searching all the passengers, especially their hand luggage. Muzzy blanched and her eyes darted wildly from face to face. Zip's father, Judge Long, had come to meet us. He was dressed in a chesterfield coat with a velvet collar and a bowler hat and looked very official. Muzzy's eyes rested for a split second on the imposing Judge but she thought better of her idea. It wasn't cricket, she knew, to use the law to break the law.

Then her eyes fell on Avis and me and lighted up happily. We would carry the bottles in our coats, she announced. No decent inspector would frisk a minor, she reasoned. We were not so sure.

Besides I pointed out that I had my hands full with a large cage full of exotic birds I had bought in Paris.

"We'll let the Judge carry them," she said. The cage

was covered with cloth and had only a slit in the top for the handle, and Judge Long had no idea what was in it when I handed it to him.

As we approached the exit where the inspectors were searching everyone coming through, Avis and I trembled with fear as the bottles jangled against each other in the pockets of the coats we carried over our arms. The crowds were jammed together and we formed a single file, Muzzy in the lead, Judge Long next and Avis and I directly behind him. Afraid that the fragile package he was carrying might be crushed by the crowds, the Judge lifted it over his head. There was a wild flapping of wings and anguished twitters as the birds found themselves turned upside down. Then the birdbath overturned and a stream of water poured out over the Judge. A trickle of birdseed followed, settling on the damp bowler and the velvet collar. I was speechless with horror but the customs inspector let out a whoop of laughter at the staid old gentleman with birdseed raining down on him. Without so much as a glance from the inspector Avis and I slipped past. Muzzy was waiting, beaming with joy, on the far side of the barrier. Once again she had done the customs inspectors in the eye.

As we children one by one left Kyneton, Muzzy's travels became less of an organized mass movement, and Muzzy herself became even more casual and if possible vaguer as she jetted around the globe. She had always been a poor sailor and the mere smell of a transatlantic liner was enough to make her feel sick. So when the airplane was introduced, she took to it as enthusiastically as she had to the Model T. She was in her eighties when she decided to fly out to Moscow to visit Avis, whose husband was Ambassador there. She had been there once visiting me before the war but she wanted to see it again. She had got as far as Amsterdam, where she went to the ladies' room in the airport to wash up after the long all-night hop across the ocean. As she combed her disorderly hair in front of the mirror, a loudspeaker bellowed:

"Mrs. Thayer please come to Gate 8. Your plane is ready for loading."

Muzzy listened vaguely and went on with her toilet.

A few moments later the speaker bellowed again:

"Mrs. Thayer please come to Gate 8 at once. Your plane to Moscow is ready for immediate departure." Again Muzzy listened but continued to straighten up her clothes.

After a third announcement a frantic air-line hostess burst into the ladies' room, found Muzzy and hustled her out to the plane just as the doors were about to close.

Later Muzzy told Avis, "You know, I was just so amazed that there were two Mrs. Thayers at Amsterdam at the same time and both of them going to Moscow!"

She had a splendid time in Moscow. Unable to speak a word of the language, she wandered about wherever she wanted to go, unperturbed by the talk of Stalin's new terror stalking the streets or by the shouts of angry policemen when she wandered into forbidden places. Her only moment of panic came when she went to the hairdresser at the National Hotel and discovered he was an old man with a long white beard.

"I was so worried he'd get the beard mixed in with my hair curlers," she said, apologizing for her timidity.

She also found the diplomatic circuit a bit disconcerting at times. One night she dined at the Italian Embassy and was seated next to the Ambassador. Afterward, driving home with Avis, she said in a small puzzled voice, "Tell me, dear, does the Italian Ambassador always pat his neighbor's knee under the table?"

On her way back from Moscow, Muzzy visited me in Munich and then flew home by way of Paris, where she had to change planes. Lest she go to ground again in the ladies' room at Orly, I asked a friend in Paris if she would keep an eye on her. The friend, the wife of an American general, apparently took no chances with Muzzy. When Muzzy got home, she wrote me about her departure from Paris. An admiral and a general had escorted her to the plane.

"There was even a red carpet," she wrote, "and a silver chain to keep the crowds back." It was almost like old times when the upper class was still on top.

TEN

Grounded

THE ALMY GRANDCHILDREN were playing in their barn when a friend of their parents' came by. They had tied a rope to the ridgepole between the two lofts, which were filled with hay. From the gloom of one loft a figure appeared clinging to the rope, swung above the cavernous barn floor and disappeared in the loft on the other side.

"Come up and join us," Charlie Almy called to the visitor. The visitor shuddered and said he was too old to play Tarzan.

A moment later another figure swung out of the gloom far above the visitor's head. Did he see wisps of white hair streaming out behind as the figure arched over the canyon below?

"There goes Grandmother," a voice from above jeered. "She's seventy-five."

On Muzzy's eightieth birthday she asked for only two presents—a wheelbarrow and a portable radio. She needed the wheelbarrow, she told us, to help John Nagle in the garden. "He's getting on," she said, though he was several years her junior, "and he just can't keep up with the weeds." She wanted the portable, she added, so that she could listen to the Phillies ball games while she did her outdoor chores. Besides weeding, the chores included pruning the trees, picking the fruit and burning off the pastures, now that there were no longer any horses or cattle to keep them cropped.

Burning the grass was one of her favorite pastimes because it was so exciting. She always waited for a long dry spell when the grass was like tinder. Then when the first strong wind came along, she went out in the fields armed with matches and her portable radio. She lit a sheaf of dry grass and dragged it around in a circle, setting fire to as large an area as she dared. Then she sat down and listened to the Phillies as the flames encircled her. The object of the game was to see how far she could let the flames grow and still put them out. Usually John Nagle smelt the first clouds of smoke and rushed to the rescue, much to her irritation, as outside help was against the rules of the game. Then the two of them would beat the grass with brooms—she inside, he outside—until eventually she escaped.

But occasionally things got completely out of hand and John had to call the Fire Department. After a while the local fire marshal made it a rule to patrol around

Kyneton during droughts when he suspected Muzzy was in a grass-burning mood. Since she hated calling attention to herself and her games, the fire marshal's patrols and the scoldings he gave her eventually put an end to the grass-burning.

As children we had always helped pick the fruit in the orchard and when we were gone the grandchildren took our places. Both generations hated the picking season chiefly because Muzzy reserved the highest and heaviest-laden branches for herself, leaving us to scavenge the lower, poorer branches. She was older, more experienced and knew the strength of her trees better than we did, she explained. When eventually the grandchildren got wise enough to avoid the orchard during picking season, she had the trees to herself. But by then the trees were old and half rotten and occasionally she misjudged the strength of a branch and came crashing out of the tree into the grass. Then one day while she was picking cherries, she fell from a high branch and broke her wrist. Her brittle old bones refused to knit properly and her wrist set crooked. Only then did we manage to persuade her to leave the picking to the birds.

It was the same way with athletics. When she was in her late sixties, George had persuaded her to leave the backfield. But she insisted on playing end. She never consented to play in the line. That was only for small children and novices.

Previous to the cherry-tree episode she had already broken her wrist several times playing hockey and at last the doctors had ordered her to play only goalie. But when the puck came near her, she never missed a chance to leave her post and charge headlong up the dump to the enemy's goal.

George's heart trouble put an end to the football and real-estate developers put an end to the dump. But tennis continued. At seventy-three Muzzy beat me 6–love in the last set of tennis I ever played. (I was thirty-seven at the time.) But then one day she herself was beaten by an athletic grandchild and soon after, following her final crash from the cherry tree, she stopped playing. Unused, the old court began to disintegrate. One afternoon our cousin George Packard came to tea and, standing on the front porch, stared wistfully at the weed-grown court where years before we had all played.

"Cousin Gertrude," he said suddenly. "I've just built a tennis court for my children and I thought it had everything a court should have. But I never thought of planting a tree on the serving line," he said, pointing to a six-foot pine that had sprouted among the weeds.

In the end Muzzy had to revert to the pedestrian old game of croquet. The croquet court by then had disappeared in a forest of lindens and beeches Muzzy and Daddy had planted fifty years before. So she decided to build a new one. This time we children were too old to help her do it herself so she persuaded the bank to let her overdraw just once more and had a contractor level off a plot in the old pasture below the tennis court.

Croquet is a cruel game at best and in Muzzy it brought out every evil instinct. She was ferocious, cunning and downright mean. When she found herself in a tight spot, she wasn't above a bit of cheating if she thought she could get away with it. Even when she was teaching her youngest grandchildren how to play, she showed no mercy. Often when the rest of us were sitting on the porch and Muzzy was playing with the grandchildren, we would hear anguished screams from the croquet court. "Please, Grandma! Don't! Please don't!" And we knew Muzzy was about to wallop a grandchild's ball out into the pasture. "They have to learn to lose," Muzzy would say when we accused her of cruelty to small children.

But what concerned us most—children, doctors and insurance agents together—was her driving. John Nagle, who had taught her to drive and had in fact been sitting beside her on the occasion of her very first crash at Pembroke gate, was crippled with rheumatism and had finally given up the wheel but Muzzy flatly refused to do any such thing.

Since she had learned to drive the Model T, cars had become faster and so had her driving. She loved power steering because with it she could take corners at full speed without any effort. Traffic on the highways had increased too in both numbers and speed. But Muzzy chose to ignore them. Most of them were out-of-towners who did not belong on our roads anyway.

She was shopping in Wayne one day with my sister Betsy, driving along the Lancaster Pike, one of the principal highways on the Main Line. Suddenly without any warning whatever she made a U turn in the face of a stream of onrushing traffic. Tires screamed and cars skidded to a stop as the drivers slammed on their brakes.

The car swayed and then righted itself. Betsy flinched and pointed to the signs forbidding U turns but Muzzy shrugged her shoulders contemptuously. "Those signs are for transients," she said placidly.

Not long afterward she crashed into a car ahead of her that, unlike Muzzy, was slowing to stop for a red light. When Fritz Drayton and Herbie Church, her insurance agents, questioned her later, she said the brakes had given out. If they wanted to scold, they should go to John Nagle. He took care of the car, not she. But from then on Muzzy kept her mishaps secret.

The excuses Muzzy gave were not always fabricated. The car she was driving was an old but fairly modern Chevrolet. John Nagle had never got much beyond the Model T stage of mechanics and when things went wrong with the more modern cars his tinkering was not always effective.

Once when I was home on vacation, I took Muzzy's car to visit some friends. On the return trip I started to slow down for a red light at the Montgomery Avenue corner but the brakes would not work and I sailed past the corner through the light, missing another car by inches, and rolled to a stop a hundred yards beyond. When I got home, I told Muzzy about my near catastrophe.

"Oh," she said casually, "that often happens to me. I must speak to John."

Some time later a neighbor called up and told Betsy, who answered the phone, that he was bringing hit-and-run charges against Muzzy. Betsy laughed a bit forcedly and said that it was quite impossible. Muzzy would never do such a thing.

"But she just did," the neighbor insisted, "and she completely demolished my left-rear fender right in front of Gane & Snyder, the butcher." Betsy again made light of it but agreed to make inquiries.

Over tea that afternoon Betsy broached the subject as gingerly as possible, asking if Muzzy had been marketing that morning. Muzzy said she had indeed.

"Was the traffic in Bryn Mawr bad?" Betsy asked.

"Not particularly."

"You had no difficulties with the car?"

Muzzy's eyes narrowed suspiciously. "Why should I? What makes you ask?"

But Betsy persisted. "You didn't by any chance hit anything, did you?"

Muzzy frowned and put on one of her most injured looks. "Of course not," she said but her voice faltered as she struggled with her conscience. "That is—well—I may have ticked a car as I drove away from Gane & Snyder," she said, her eyes wandering around the room. "Do fix those flowers," she said, pointing to a vase. "They're all lopsided."

Later Betsy called the butcher and asked if by chance he had noticed Muzzy ticking someone's car outside his store.

"Ticking?" said Mr. Snyder. "When Mrs. Thayer rammed into that car in front of her, the meat fell off the hooks in my shop."

Then Betsy called up Fritz Drayton at the insurance company and he and Herbie Church took over from there. By that time it had become a routine.

And just as she insisted on driving her car, she went right on attending to her correspondence, her bills and her household affairs. There were lapses, of course, as when she wrote a letter to one of her children and mailed it to another or when she sent her monthly plea for an advance to the butcher instead of to the bank. But Betsy kept an eye out for them.

Once the Cancer Society addressed a questionnaire to her, which she conscientiously filled out, proudly noting down her excellent health at the age of eighty-eight. Before she mailed it, Betsy managed to get a glimpse at what she had written.

To one question asking whether she had lost any teeth, she had answered with a bold "No!"

Betsy started. "What do you mean by saying you haven't lost any teeth, Muzzy?"

Muzzy bridled defiantly. "Of course I haven't," she said. "I sometimes lose my glasses but never my teeth."

But Betsy was not always around to check her vaguenesses. One day Muzzy got into her car, which had been standing in front of Kyneton, and drove down to Bryn Mawr to do the shopping. She parked in front of the grocer's, and when she had completed her marketing, a young salesboy helped her carry the parcels out to the car. As he opened the door, a large black poodle sprang at him from inside.

Annoyed that a stray dog should get into her car, Muzzy told the boy to drag the beast out. The boy reached for him but the poodle snapped at his hand. Muzzy, who was always impatient with people who couldn't manage animals, pushed him aside and ordered the dog out. Wagging its tail with delight, the poodle climbed down and jumped affectionately around Muzzy. Then she haughtily ordered the poodle on its way and drove off.

That evening Betsy came up to Kyneton for a drink and told Muzzy that Petey, her black poodle, was missing. Had Muzzy by any chance seem him?

A strange guilty look came over Muzzy's face as she remembered the dog in her car at the grocer's. In the end it cost her ten dollars to get Petey out of the Bryn Mawr dog pound.

After several more ticking incidents reported by the police in Bryn Mawr, we tried again to persuade Muzzy to give up driving but she stubbornly refused. With John no longer driving it would mean having to impose on us or her friends whenever she went out, and she was certainly not going to give up her daily visits to her children and grandchildren to say nothing of early church several times a week. We persuaded the bank to offer her a regular chauffeur. But Muzzy rejected that solution out of hand. "It would hurt John Nagle's feelings," she said and that was that. We asked the Bryn Mawr police chief to take away her license but he, an old friend of hers despite the troubles she caused, refused. It was not his business but the Commonwealth of Pennsylvania's, he explained. We wrote to the Commonwealth but they too declined to act. There was no law against Muzzy's driving, they claimed.

So we asked Fritz Drayton and Herbie Church to cancel her insurance but they also dodged the issue. Why should they destroy a lifelong friendship with a favorite cousin? But they did agree to give Muzzy a lecture on her driving. She listened impatiently and flatly denied that any of the recent accidents had been her fault. "That automatic transmission behaves so oddly," she said. "You ought to speak to John." Fritz and Herbie exchanged helpless glances and went home.

Not long afterward Fritz, who lived across the road from Kyneton, was passing the corner at Montgomery Avenue when he saw a familiar-looking car lying on its side in the ditch. He stopped to investigate and as he approached the wreck the occupant, a woman, rolled down a side window and began to climb out. Then she saw Fritz approaching and ducked back in. But when Fritz peered in at her, Muzzy knew the game was up. She stuck her head through the window again.

"Drat it! Fritz Drayton," she said impatiently. "You're the very last person in the world I wanted to see at this point."

Later she complained that the power steering was to blame. "It sometimes turns the car too sharply," she said.

In the end it was not the police chief or the Commonwealth of Pennsylvania or the insurance company who put an end to her driving but arthritis. When the pains in her legs became so bad that she could not work the pedals even when they were functioning, she herself decided to give up.

It was a very bitter decision. Now she had to wait for her children and grandchildren to come to her each day. Even worse, not just she but half a dozen friends whom she had always picked up on the way to early church were stranded. And when she went out to dinner or to play bridge, she had to order a taxi, an expense she deplored even more than the bank did. Besides it was so humiliating—like hiring McGrady in the old days to drive her in his station carriage reeking of horse sweat, chewing tobacco and McGrady.

But just because she gave up driving, Muzzy had no intention of vegetating at Kyneton and withdrawing from the Machine Age she had embraced so enthusiastically fifty years before. And when the Space Age dawned, Muzzy was out in front cheering as usual. She had read in the paper that the first Soviet Sputnik was due to pass over Kyneton one morning at 4 A.M.—a gesture from the Russians that she felt obliged to acknowledge. So she set her alarm and a few minutes before four in the morning she went out on the lawn to greet the Sputnik and cheer it on its way. She watched enthralled as the little light moved across the sky and when it finally disappeared she turned back to the house. Unfortunately in the darkness she didn't see the stump of a tree in her path and fell over it. But she managed to get up and limp into the empty old house.

Next morning her hip was an angry purple and Betsy sent for the doctor. Fearing that a blood clot might form, he ordered Muzzy to the hospital at once.

"Hospital?" Muzzy said. "Go to the hospital at my age?"

The doctor insisted but Muzzy continued to object. "Tomorrow we're having the fiftieth anniversary of the Garden Club and as the oldest member I have been asked to cut the cake."

In the end Muzzy had her way. She went to the Garden Club, cut the cake and then reluctantly entered the hospital as a patient for the first time in her life.

A day or two later I arrived home on leave at Idlewild Airport and when I telephoned to Kyneton I found out that Muzzy was at Bryn Mawr Hospital. Worried, I called her there and was relieved to hear her voice, enthusiastic if not downright ecstatic.

"If I'd only known how exciting it was being a patient," she said, "I'd have tried it ages ago."

But the hospital life soon bored her and she was back at Kyneton within a few days.

I stayed with her that summer at Kyneton and when the Fourth of July came around Muzzy insisted we raise the flag as usual. The rope on the flagpole had rotted away so I got a ladder and a tack hammer and nails while Muzzy fetched the flag from the linen closet where it was always kept.

Her arthritis was plaguing her so I pushed her out to the flagpole in her wheel chair for the ceremony. She watched solemnly while I fixed the flag to the pole, and reminded me of the days many years before when the whole family had lined up and saluted as Daddy hoisted the Stars and Stripes.

When I had finished, I said jokingly that I hoped the flag had fifty stars. Muzzy snorted impatiently. "It's the one we've always used," she said. Then I counted the stars. There were forty-five.

Because of arthritis she also had to give up her long daily walks through the woods around Kyneton, which for years she had taken to keep fit after touch football, hockey and tennis had ended. Whatever the weather, she had set forth for a brisk hour or so, wearing a leather jacket and carrying a walking stick. When she returned, her hair streamed from under her soft tweed hat, her nose was red and her cheeks pink from the bitter winds.

Now her only sports were watching baseball and football on the television or listening to them by radio. She was eighty-nine when my sister Buckety asked her to help entertain her neighbors on Chester County Antiquarians Day at the old Almy farm near Paoli. Crippled though she was, she accepted eagerly and was placed in a chair on the porch, a blanket over her legs. All afternoon long she held forth to the visitors who streamed through the house about the outdoor fireplace and other historical features around her.

But late in the afternoon Buckety noticed that she seemed tense and drawn. She came to ask her how she felt and as she leaned over the chair she heard the murmur of a radio coming from under the blanket. She asked Muzzy how things were going.

"Badly," Muzzy snapped. "Yankees leading. It's the top of the ninth, bases loaded, two down, and a full count on Snyder."

Muzzy did not confine her baseball vocabulary to the game only. When an English cousin wrote to ask if he might come and stay a few days at Kyneton, he was thoroughly mystified when he got a reply from Muzzy regretfully putting him off with the cryptic explanation that "the Wainmans are presently at bat, the Bohlens are on deck and the Zanes are in the circle."

Confined to her chair, she spent much of her time watching her favorite Phillies. She knew the name of every player on the team, his batting average, his strengths and his weaknesses. She scolded and groaned and pounded her fist on the table when they erred, and smiled and cheered when they did well.

After years "in the cellar," the Phillies had suddenly revived in 1964 and to her joy reached a pinnacle that even she in all her years of following them had never known—the top of the league. It was her final triumph for by the time their luck changed and they dropped back she was no longer watching.

Except for occasional visitors Muzzy was living all alone at Kyneton. The old servants, Lizzy and John, Bridget and Augustus, Maggie, Louise and Sarah had all died or retired. A Negro couple with two small children were looking after "the back" and a team of efficient and cheerful nurses took care of her as she entered her nineties.

Now as she sat each afternoon in the big chair behind

the tea table, she seemed tiny and very fragile. As her mind grew vaguer, it seemed to dwell mostly on her childhood and she often confused her children with her sisters and brothers, all long since gone. What she enjoyed most was when her twenty-two grandchildren and twelve great-grandchildren came in droves to tea, dashing about noisily and gobbling the cakes and sandwiches just as we had done a half century before at Pembroke, her childhood home. With the children she was always bright and alert, teasing and playing games and still trying her best to win.

When there were no grandchildren or great-grandchildren, there were always Binky and Adie, the children of the couple in "the back," to keep her company and entertain her.

On Halloween evening they and their parents decorated the drawing room with pumpkin heads and candles. The father, who was butler, served dinner before the fireplace dressed as a Mohammedan sheik. His wife helped, dressed as an Oriental princess. The two children were made up as goblins with ferocious-looking masks.

After dinner the two children, joined by a few neighbors, made the rounds of nearby houses for "trick or treat." Well supplied with candies, apples and cake, Muzzy received them warmly and entered into their pranks with verve. In fact the reception was so warm that word quickly spread through the neighborhood that the old lady on the hill was receiving. Soon the big room was full of children all pretending to be goblins or witches while Muzzy cowered and cried out in fright at their fierce antics. She played the role of a terrified old lady so convincingly that Binky took pity on her and, sidling up to her chair, he raised his mask.

"Don't be scared, Grandmuzzy," he whispered. "It's only me. Just Binky."

As the nurse helped her to bed that evening, Muzzy said, "That was the nicest Halloween I've ever had." It was her last.

ABOUT THE AUTHOR

Charles W. Thayer was born in 1910, the fifth of six children of George and Gertrude Thayer, at Kyneton, Villanova, Pennsylvania, where he spent his childhood. He went to Kyneton School, Haverford School and St. Paul's School. After a year off in Europe he went to West Point, from which he graduated in 1933. He then resigned from the Regular Army and joined the United States Foreign Service. For twenty years he served around the world, chiefly in Russia and Germany.

During the war, he became a parachutist and served as American liaison officer to Tito. Subsequently he served as a political adviser to General Mark Clark in Austria and as a member of the joint U.S.–U.S.S.R. Commission in Korea.

After the war he returned to the Foreign Service, reorganized the Voice of America and served as United States liaison officer to Adenauer's first government in Bonn. His last post was as Consul General in Munich, Germany.

In 1953 he resigned to devote himself to writing. His books include: *Bears in the Caviar, Hands Across the Caviar, The Unquiet Germans, Diplomat, Russia* (with the editors of *Life*), *Guerrilla,* and two novels—*Moscow Interlude* and *Checkpoint.*

At present he divides his time between his home, Clover Mill House in Chester Springs, Pennsylvania, not far from Kyneton, and his shooting lodge in Bavaria.